FORGOTTEN IS THE NAME

The fascinating story of the extraordinary adventures, life, and ministry of Reverend Ulysses S. Grant Perkins

Paul M. Perkins

*There were footprints on the hill
and men lie buried under,
Tamers of the earth and rivers,
They died at the end of labor,
Forgotten is the name.*
                    Stephen Vincent Benet*

*See footnote 88

FAIRWAY PRESS
DRAWER L • LIMA, OHIO 45802

FORGOTTEN IS THE NAME

FIRST EDITION
Copyright © 1985 by
Fairway Press
Lima, Ohio

All rights reserved. No portion of this book may be reproduced or utilized in any form or by any means, electronic or mechanical including photocopying, without permission in writing from the publisher. Inquiries should be addressed to: Fairway Press, Drawer L, Lima, Ohio 45802.

7574 / ISBN 0-89536-938-9   PRINTED IN U.S.A.

*Dedicated to the memory of
Blossom McDade Perkins
1908-1982*

"She dressed her soul in blouse and sandals"

Contents

Photo Index	7
Preface	9
1. Birth and Beginning	11
2. A Gathering at Buck's	18
3. Methodist Circuit Rider	24
4. Life in a Log Cabin	29
5. The Youth's Companion	33
6. A Photograph of 1886	38
7. Appearance in a Garden	41
8. Army Volunteer	44
9. Fort Sully, South Dakota	49
10. Fort "Swift Water"	54
11. Mountain College	60
12. Cavalry Captain	66
13. The Valedictory	72
14. Diary of a Voyage	75
15. Traveler in Europe	83
16. Leipzig University	86
17. The Bishop and the Student	91
18. The Passing of the Alps	94
19. 38 Via Firenze, Rome	98
20. Pilgrimage	102
21. In the Holy Land	107
22. On Horseback to Jerusalem	110
23. Jerusalem	116
24. Bachelor Minister	123
25. Victorine	129
26. Moving to Michigan	133
27. The Roosevelt Vatican Incident	138
28. Other Than Theology	142
29. Five Dollars a Day	146
30. Death and a Memory	149
31. Life Goes On	154

32. Public Issues of 1917......................... 160
33. YMCA Hut at Camp Sherman.................. 164
34. Antioch College 1919......................... 169
35. Normalcy 1920............................... 173
36. "Hardscrabble Hellas"....................... 178
37. The Final Years.............................. 183
Epilogue.. 188
Footnotes 190

Index of Photographs

No.	Description	Pg.
1.	Perkins mountain kin taken about 1910 by Grant. He was an early camera buff. I have many of his original negatives and his 1900 Brownie.	23
2.	Grant's father, Dempsey White Perkins, the Methodist circuit rider, about 1870.	28
3.	Elizabeth Sharp Perkins, Grant's mother.	28
4.	Private Ulysses S. G. Perkins, 1892.	48
5.	Soldiers drilling at Fort Niobrara, Nebraska, about 1890.	58
6.	Sioux Indians dancing at Fort Niobrara, July 4, 1889.	59
7.	Fort Niobrara from the bluff.	59
8.	Fanny Henning Speed, wife of Joshua Speed, Abraham Lincoln's best friend and benefactor of Union College.	65
9.	James P. Faulkner, Grant's cousin, and President of Union College in 1901.	65
10.	Captain U.S.G. Perkins, Spanish War, 1898.	71
11.	Grant Perkins as a student in Germany in 1905	81
12.	Dutch steamship, Statendam, 1905.	82
13.	The Methodist Center, 38 Via Firenza, Rome, 1905.	101
14.	The French steamship, Memfi, at Messina enroute to Alexandria, February, 1906.	106

15.	Jerusalem inside the Damascus Gate, 1906.	114
16.	A Bedouin camp on the road to Jericho, 1906.	114
17.	Bedouin boys in the Kidron Valley, February, 1906.	115
18.	Camel outside the Jaffa Gate, Jerusalem, March, 1906.	120
19.	Mount of Olives from the bridge, March, 1906.	121
20.	The Damascus Gate, Jerusalem, March, 1906.	121
21.	The Via Dolorosa, Jerusalem, March, 1906.	122
22.	Trinity Methodist Church, Latonia, Kentucky, Grant's first church. It was later moved and became a movie house.	128
23.	The same, interior. Note the heating stove.	128
24.	Victorine McDaniel about 1907.	132
25.	Grant on the lake steamer, Alpena, moving to Michigan, September, 1909.	137
26.	Victorine on the same steamer.	137
27.	Victorine's last picture, 1914, with her two sons.	153
28.	Grant and Lyla Maxfield, Brutus, Michigan.	158
29.	Grant and his 1916 Model T Ford	159
30.	Grant at Camp Sherman, Ohio, as a Y man, 1918.	168
31.	The Horace Mann home at Antioch College, about 1890.	172

A Preface About Ordinary People

The stories of the ordinary people are not often told. There are many celebrities remembering trivia or telling bedroom stories; but mainly the ordinary people, walking quietly through their lives, are those who keep our society and nation glued together.

We only see ordinary people in glimpses. In a local history, even though the story is most often told in the flowery language of that genre. In a soldier's fragment about an old battle. Or in the crumbling pages of a diary about a part of a life. It was such a diary of my father that became both the starting point and motivation for this book.

I use the word ordinary only in the sense that such people are unknown. There are many extraordinary people among the ordinary, but discovering the details of their lives is often difficult, if not impossible.

Still, a sensitive geologist of man can often find the minute traces made by the ordinary people; and in those faint signatures and echoes of stilled voices, he can truly explore the rich strata of the human spirit. Even though faintly and awkwardly, ordinary people do write their signatures on their times.

My father, Ulysses S. Grant Perkins (1873-1936), looked down on most men from the top of a six foot three inch Kentucky mountain oak frame. He was not born to much promise or hope in a two-room log house in Whitley County, Kentucky. But his story — orphan, itinerant farm hand, a soldier around the Indian reservations in the West, mountain college, cavalry captain in the Spanish War in 1898, seminary student, traveler to Europe and Palestine in 1905, and Methodist minister — is interesting and worth telling.

When he enlisted in the army he was Ulysses S. G. Perkins. But he must have hated that name. Later he simplified it to Grant.

He responded vigorously to the now forgotten public issues of the swift and tumultuous late nineteenth and early twentieth centuries. The big events — the wars, the depressions, and the metamorphosis of America into an industrial from an agricultural nation — he felt and saw personally and not from the questionable omniscience of history.

Even though he was unimportant in the hierarchy of his church, he was important to me, to his family, and to the small Methodist congregations he served. But most of all he was important to himself. He took pride in his life and career and tried to know both God and Man. Whether we are great or small, this is the truest test of human dignity and worth.

I have wanted to tell his story ever since as a young man I first became aware of the color and adventure in his life. But this book had to wait the completion of a professional career and the raising of a family. Someday, I always told myself, I will do this. I am glad someday has arrived, not too late. At seventy plus, I have become aware of the end of time, at least on earth.

                                    Paul M Perkins
                                    Minerva, Ohio
                                    1985

Chapter One
Birth And Beginning

The March night was cold, but an extra log in the fireplace drove most of the frost out of the big room in the log house. The midwife, or Granny, thin and bent, went about her work silently and efficiently, with only a few directions to Dempsey Perkins, the anxious but helpless father.

She had delivered scores of babies in Meadowcreek Valley and knew how to deal with worried and bumbling fathers — by banishing them. In 1873 there were no doctors in the mountains of Kentucky to take care of the astounding increase in population taking place in that state.

The firelight danced uncertainly on the log walls. The only sounds were the sharp cries of Elizabeth, Dempsey's wife, and the quiet words of encouragement of the midwife. Dempsey's father, John Felix Perkins, called Buck, had come from the next valley. But he was banished also, for the midwife's word was law.

Banished also were Elizabeth's five other sons. Benjamin Franklin, 12, already called Rod for his hickory whip thin body. Felix, 9, later to be called Uncle Fudd. And Joseph, William, and George, ranging from seven to two years of age. Unable to sleep, they listened from the loft, reached by a ladder, where they had their beds of straw ticks, as the universal ritual of birth was played out.

Soon it was over, and the cabin bustled with grandparents, aunts, and cousins of various kinds. Since about 1814, this was the fourth generation of the clan Perkins to live in this part of the Meadowcreek Valley.

So Ulysses S. Grant Perkins was born March 10, 1873.

General Ulysses S. Grant had been re-elected President of the United States the previous November. That the sixth and last son of Dempsey and Elizabeth Perkins was so named was a measure of General Grant's stature in the primitive home of this intense Methodist Circuit rider.

What were this land and people into which Grant Perkins was born? Both deeply affected his life. First, the land. Meadowcreek Valley is in Whitley County, Kentucky, which lies on the Tennessee border. As one of nineteen counties embracing a crumpled bastion of rough hills officially known as The Cumberland Plateau, it is more familiarly known as the Kentucky Mountains. These are, in turn, a part of a larger mountain swath in parts of Maryland, West Virginia, Virginia, Tennessee, Kentucky, North and South Carolina, Georgia and Alabama, now called The Appalachians.

Creeks have always had a unique place in these mountains. Before there were roads, the creek valleys were the easiest way to get in and out of the mountains. Even today, one can find a family more easily than in any other way by the creek valley in which they live. Even the land grant records at the capitol in Frankfort are described only by name, acreage, county, and creek. The creeks were often named for some feature about them or event on them. Dead Man, Defeated, Greasy, Stinking, Yellow, Cotton, Jack's Fork, Lynn Camp, and Elk are names of creeks in Whitley County today.

The creeks were also useful in a surprising way. When Dempsey, Grant's father, would ride into Williamsburg, the county seat, part of the road just dropped into the shale-bottomed, dry creek bed. Under the leafy shade of the maples and oaks for several miles, this was the road. Only in 1945 did the county get that road out of the creek bed.

Meadowcreek Valley was also only ten miles away from another famous road — The Wilderness Road. From the east, the early settlers had poured through the Cumberland Gap twenty five miles southeast of Meadowcreek Valley on The Wilderness Road. This great western road wound up through Knox County, only a few miles away. It was the way Grant's great-great-grandfather Jabez had come from the North Carolina mountains in 1810.

Before 1803, The Wilderness Road had been almost the

only practical immigration and trade route from the east to the bursting west. From Maryland, it had followed the valleys lying between the Blue Ridge and Allegheny Mountains pointing southwest, and then turned northwest through the Cumberland Gap to the bluegrass plains of Kentucky. The easy route down the Ohio and Mississippi Rivers was blocked by the French control over Louisiana.

After the Louisiana Purchase by President Thomas Jefferson in 1803, The Wilderness Road declined in importance. During the Civil War, it had become an almost impassable trace of broken bridges, washouts, and deep ruts. So bad that General Grant, in a personal inspection, vetoed it as a route to invade the South.

Thus by 1873, growing America had simply flowed around and had not penetrated the inner valleys of the mountains. Lacking roads, commerce, or railroads, the people of the mountains were a mystery to most Americans. They lived, as did the family that Grant Perkins was born into, in self-sufficient tribes or clusters in profound isolation from the main streams of American life. In 1873 life and language were mostly frozen in the state that had existed at the beginning of the nineteenth century.

The land was almost awesome in its beauty. Its hardwood forests were thick with oak, maple, and towering poplars. Its streams ran clear, filled with fish. The farming was a harsh life, but bottom lands were fertile to the touch of the plow. In 1873 neither the eastern coal corporations, nor the timber barons, nor the railroads had yet come to Whitley County. So the picture of the miserable cabins clustered around a coal tipple, as shown in the opening scenes of *The Coal Miner's Daughter* movie, was not yet the life of the Kentucky mountains.

What of the Perkins family? Grant's father, Dempsey, was in 1873 a farmer and a Methodist circuit-riding minister, already troubled by tuberculosis which would take his life in two years. His grandfather John Felix, or Buck, was a substantial landowner in the valley. His great grandfather, Solomon, had been one of the first settlers on Meadowcreek in 1814. His great-great-grandfather, Jabez, had emigrated from the North Carolina mountains to another part of the county even before that.

In later years Grant, aware that families are without start and without end, would try to find out more about his. Its pioneer flavor, much like that of thousands of American families, would stir his interest but he will never even discover the name of his ancestor Jabez.

His family history in America actually began with Edward Perkins, the younger son of an innkeeper and farmer in Hillmorton Parish, County Warwick, England, who arrived in the Puritan colony of New Haven, Connecticut, before 1646. It was the height of the Puritan exodus from England. Three generations of Edward's descendants lived around settled and civilized New Haven until about 1774, when two brothers, Timothy and Joseph, left New Haven for the wild and dangerous mountains of North Carolina.

Tradition says that Timothy and Joseph Perkins were tax collectors in New Haven, and had run into a fierce buzz saw of opposition to English taxes, even though the stamp tax had been repealed a year after its passage without the collection of any tax. But Timothy and Joseph then became the historic Tories of old Wilkes County, North Carolina.

They sent their wives and children by sailing ship from New Haven to the mouth of the Cape Fear River, near what is now Wilmington, North Carolina. Among the children was Grant's great-great-grandfather Jabez. The men and their pack animals came down the Wilderness Road, cradled in the Shenandoah River Valley, a road which pointed southwest into the dark unknown.

In 1774 the upper part of the Wilderness Road was rapidly being settled. They had to stop at William Inglis's ferry across the New River, near what is now Radford, Virginia. South of that river the Wilderness Road had been only opened after treaties in 1768 with the Cherokee Indians at Fort Stanwiz, and was only a slash of cut trees in the dense forest.

At Inglis's they heard the story of a Shawnee raid at Draper's Meadows many years before when Inglis's wife and small son had been kidnapped. His wife had escaped and had heroically found her way back from the Shawnee Camp on the Ohio River. But the son had only recently been found and ransomed. For years he had grown up as the adopted son of a Shawnee chief, knowing only Indian ways and language.

At Inglis's they also learned of an area called Old Fields, lying about sixty miles up near the headwaters of the New River. There by some fluke of nature the grasses and not the forest had taken over, leaving six thousand acres of clear meadow land. These fields were *old* corn fields of the Indians.

So Timothy Perkins and his party had abandoned their plans for going farther west and settled on Old Fields in North Carolina near the Virginia border. Four years after, in April, 1778, Timothy "Purkins" made a land entry in newly formed Wilkes County of 400 acres where the Gap Creek enters the South Fork of the New River. These had been Crown lands which the State of North Carolina had taken over in the Confiscation Act earlier that year.

The Revolutionary War spread to Wilkes County in 1781 when British General Cornwallis penetrated to Guilford Courthouse, near the Virginia border in his southern campaign. From there he made his fatal move to Yorktown where he was trapped and surrendered. Timothy and his brother Joseph served in the British militia in South Carolina, probably to insulate their families from the heat of war, which, in the mountains of North Carolina, was as much a civil war as it was a war for independence.

Near the cabin of Timothy Perkins on April 14, 1781, and during his absence, Tory Captain Riddle ambushed and captured Colonel Benjamin Cleveland, a North Carolina militia officer. Cleveland later escaped, and in turn captured Riddle, summarily executing him. In the mountain country no quarter was asked or given on either side. Timothy, fighting on the Tory side, lost his life in a skirmish at Old Fields before 1783.

But Grant will never know these stories of his ancestors during his lifetime. In the mountains (as, indeed, among most families in America) such knowledge never extended farther back than two or three generations. Yet, as wave upon wave penetrated the continent, there must be tens of thousands of similar sagas in the families and lives of ordinary Americans. Their stories are lost in the mists of the real history of our land. Forgotten are the names.

Two aspects of these beginnings deeply affected Grant's

life. First, Timothy and his children were not just like some mountain pioneers, primitive hunters who followed the game and lived like the Indians. In settled and civilized New Haven, he had known laws and land titles. By the early 1800's Timothy's children had acquired over 5300 acres in North Carolina and in a neighboring county in Virginia, and were described in one footnote as all wealthy.

Jabez, son of Timothy, and the ancestor who came to Kentucky, sold lands in Grayson County, Virginia, for one thousand dollars (a large amount in that day), while he was already in Kentucky in 1813. He also had lands in Illinois. John Felix (Buck), Grant's grandfather, with four hundred acres, a legal still for whiskey, a blacksmith shop, had the same acquisitive instincts.

In his early life, this was important to Grant, whose father Dempsey died when the boy was only two, for Buck and Buck's brother Timothy gave fifty acres of their land to the widow Elizabeth for the support of her family of six boys. This strong family support — typical in the isolated mountains — was his security base when Grant was growing up.

The second aspect of his ancestral soil that would be influential in Grant's life was the long tradition of the Methodist church in his family. In 1736 Timothy had been baptized in the Congregational Church of the Puritans in New Haven, Connecticut, but the Puritans never followed the settlers into the mountains. And so, with marching orders perhaps from Bishop Francis Asbury himself, some now nameless Methodist circuit preacher must have touched some of the children of Timothy.

In 1828, Dr. Elisha Mitchell (a Presbyterian who did not approve of some of the ways of the Methodists) visited the home of Timothy Perkins Jr. on Helton Creek, in Ashe County, North Carolina, and went to a Methodist meeting there. He wrote: "After the meeting I staid for a class meeting and heard a reasonable amount of female screaming and vociferation."[1] The Weekly Class Meeting was an early, and now mostly discarded, feature of that church. Its function was to keep close tabs on the behavior of its members. It is almost certain that Solomon Perkins, Grant's great-grandfather, brought the Methodist faith with him into the mountains in 1814.

Today, the cabin which was the site of the opening scene in this chapter has long since disappeared. Nothing is left except a pile of field stones which once stood as a chimney for the fireplace. The spring where Grant carried water for his mother is still there. In the woods on a hill overlooking the site are the graves of Dempsey and Elizabeth Perkins. Green myrtle covers the untended graves.

Many sounds now drift up Meadowcreek Valley on a warm summer's day. The barking of a dog. The bell of a thin cow wandering in the woods. The wind rustling the corn in the bottom field where Grant worked so often as a boy. Except for the absence of the huge hardwoods of the primeval forest, nothing has changed. One can stand there and see a hundred years into the past.

A newer house stands not far away. When its residents heard there was a graveyard on top of the hill, "They 'lowed they never knowed a grave yard was up thar." Such is the profound anonymity of those buried there.[2]

Chapter Two

A Gathering At Buck's

The oak and maple leaves drenched the hillsides of Meadowcreek Valley in brown and scarlet in the autumn of 1860. Dempsey Perkins was trying to finish the cabin before winter for his bride and himself. Wiping the sweat from his browned face, he stopped to rest and drink from the rock spring. Inside, the bark had been peeled from the new green logs, and they smelled fresh and sweet.

He tested the new clay mud of the field stone chimney. He was especially proud of two real glass windows. The door swung silently on its leather hinges. The puncheon floor (oak slabs with the flat side up laid directly on the earth) was clean and yet little used. He knocked out the heavy skids by which the upper logs had been hoisted into place and went in to supper.

His wife Elizabeth, born to John and Sarah Sharp on Jack's Fork in Knox County only 10 miles away, was preparing their meal. In the glow of bridehood, each heavy wooden pail from the spring was a light load for her. Each supper of salt pork and corn bread and burnt coffee was a feast of love. But her new life was really not new at all, simply an extension of her girlhood. Looming, choring, cooking, hoeing, sewing, spinning, cutting firewood, waiting on men folk, and looking for ginseng (that wild herb the outside world would pay cash for) was all that she had known all her life.

At twenty-one in the spring of life, these were no burdens. But she had seen how many of her aunts and neighbors were old women at forty. They sank into the harsh and stagnant life. It was women's lot, that's all. But at John and Sarah

Sharp's cabin things were quite different. Nine Sharp girls (Sharp both in name and spirit) brightened the neighborhood. Their very names were chosen by the poets — Louisa, Polly, Indiana, Elzira, Emily Mandeville, Sarah Emeline, Samantha Madeline, Jane Bosket and Grant's mother, Elizabeth Winburn.

Born in 1799, Sarah Sharp outlived most of her own children to age ninety-seven. As a girl in Virginia she had learned money in the form of shillings and pounds, currency which even survived the Revolution. Even late in life, she thought in those terms but was able to change these instantly into dollars and cents — a living computer.

Dempsey was prepared for winter. The corn was either in the log barn or over at his father Buck's still to be made into whiskey, a cash crop. He had some tough razor-back hogs. But before they would be slaughtered and their meat salted down, they would be led into a separate corn field for fattening. This was called "hoggin' down a corn field". Families were judged in this. As Grant's cousin Ernest Perkins once put it, "Never no family makin' less than four hogs hardly worth a damn."

Hides had been taken to the shoemaker at Williamsburg for shoes. Dried beans on their long stalks, potatoes, and salt pork slabs filled the small storage or "plunder" room. The vital stack of winter cord-wood was growing.

Dempsey and Elizabeth were excited about the next day. His father, John Felix or Buck, was having a "gatherin' " at his double log house in the next valley. Neighbors and kinfolk had been invited for some sport, vittles, "black betty" (whiskey) for the men, gossip for the women, and exchange of news for all. It was an annual event that Grant remembered as a boy.

Elizabeth was looking forward to seeing her sister Samantha, whom she had not seen since her marriage to Frank Faulkner in 1859. Nor had she seen others of her family since her marriage to Dempsey, even though they only lived ten miles away. Even a ten mile trip on foot or horseback over old buffalo trails, often grown shut with laural and brush, was a hard thing.

The next day they walked over the hill, on whose top they

will later rest in their graves, into the next valley where Dempsey had been born and raised. Most of his eight older brothers and sisters still lived around Meadowcreek. His uncle Timothy, his cousins Hardin, Arch, and Crackett Dunham, and his aunts Patsy Owens and Mary Polly Brown, arrived to excited greetings, their children all swarming together like bees.

A tall bearded patriarch, Buck greeted his neighbors and kinfolk. As owner of 400 acres of land, a still, and a blacksmith shop, he was a well-to-do man by mountain standards. He liked to turn his cash income into gold coins. When his children married he gave each a generous handful.

Buck was a religious man without being a very kind man. His grandson Ernest says he would beat his sons John, James, and Jeff every Saturday for all the unknown sins they had committed during the week. John and James were aware of their own sins but knew that Jeff never did anything wrong. As angry boys they told Buck that if he ever beat Jeff again, they would kill him. The old man knew the threat was real. He never beat Jeff again.

The men went off to a nearby field for some shooting, priming their muzzle-loading rifles for the targets. They were all crack shots. After, they went to a large pile of corn near the log barn for a corn shucking contest, with the prize a "black betty" or jug of corn whiskey in the center of the pile.

Another contest was the breaking of the oak spikes, a familiar logging tool. One form of cash crop then came in the form of the big hardwoods from the forests. Primitive logging could only take place near the creeks that flowed into the Cumberland River. With oxen, the big logs were snaked down the dangerous hill slopes to the creek banks to await the spring floods. Timothy, Grant's great uncle, was usually the winner of the breaking of the spikes, cracking the iron-like wood over his knee.

Elizabeth joyfully embraced her sister Samantha and admired her baby boy of two months, who would later become Judge Henry Cook Faulkner of Hazard, Kentucky.

Before supper, the men talked politics. Secession was in the air but fiercely opposed in the mountains. Even though the new Republican Party and Abraham Lincoln were not making an impression in the hills, (Lincoln only got six votes in Whitley County in 1860), Stephen Douglas and the regular Democrats were doing little better with fourteen. Most of the Whitley County votes went to Kentuckian Breckinridge.[3]

Before a bright and warming fire after supper, they asked Frank Faulkner to tell the story of his travels. Tucked into the folds of their mothers's skirts, the children fell asleep. The others listened to tales that for them must have been from outer space.

In 1847, Frank Faulkner had married Emily Sharp, Elizabeth's older sister. Emily had died only a few months later. Frank had then gone to Missouri where his uncle James lived. During the Mexican War he had joined a grain convoy bound for the American army in Mexico. In 1849 he helped organize a train of twenty-five wagons and a hundred Kentuckians going to the Gold Rush in California. With his slave Sam, they had been the hunters for the train.

To his entranced audience he described the scenes at Independence, Missouri, the jumping-off place, with its hundreds of canvas-covered wagons, organized as military columns. He painted the turbulent Missouri, the white-sanded Platte, the endless plains, the vast herds of buffalo, the Sweetwater Pass skirting peaks of never melting snow, the lurking Indians, the hot deserts, the hostile Mormons (who often imprisoned those passing through their lands), the feared Sierra Mountains which one must pass before the snows came, the crazed excitement for gold in California, the wages and prices hardly to be believed (a dollar for an egg), and a majestic waterfall a half mile high in the Yosemite Valley. He always claimed to be the first white man to have seen that valley.[4] He may have been, for the first recorded and organized penetration was by Major James Savage who was sent into it in 1851 to move the Uzamite Indians to a reservation.[5]

He told of living of the insane tumult in San Francisco and of taking a steamer to the Sandwich Islands, or Hawaii, where he found the missionaries controlled the islands, King and all. From Hawaii, he had written to Samantha Sharp, the sister of his deceased wife, Emily. One day she was astonished to get a letter postmarked Sydney, Australia. He had then returned again to San Francisco from the Hawaiian Islands.

He once said that if he were a rich man, he would live in California and have a home in the Sandwich Islands. Frank Faulkner was a jet-setter born in the wrong century.

He had come home to Kentucky across Panama, then called New Granada, where enterprising Americans had built a railroad across the isthmus to cash in on the thousands of gold seekers wishing to cut short a sea voyage around South America.

He may have heard of an event in 1856 which has a modern ring, the first anti-American riot, triggered by a drunken American who would not pay for a melon.[6] His ship had stopped at Acapulco where he had watched Mexican boys dive for coins in the clear green waters. From New York he came by rail to Lexington, and to Barbourville by stage, bringing a wedding dress from California for Samantha.

The fire had died down and the hour was late when Frank Faulkner finished his story. That he stirred the imaginations and longings of his listeners is clear when one considers what happened to some of Dempsey's brothers, sisters, and cousins who had heard Frank Faulkner's astounding story.

Mary married a Foster and went to Nevada. Eliza married Ladd Allen and went to Oregon. Emily married Jim Grant and went to Nebraska to claim land opened up by the Homestead Act of 1862. Frank Faulkner had pierced the dark isolation of the mountains with a thin laser thread of dazzling light about the outside world.

*1. Mountain kinfolk about 1910
(Photo by Grant Perkins)*

Chapter Three

Methodist Circuit Rider

Dempsey kicked his horse as he rode along the forest trail, hoping for a little more speed. The oak leaves had not yet been painted bright brown, for the long September summer still lingered. He was impatient to tell his wife Elizabeth the exciting news. The 1869 Conference of the Methodist Episcopal Church North had accepted him on trial as an itinerant preacher, his territory, the Booneville Kentucky Circuit of more than fifteen counties.

But his horse knew his own speed; and after a few quickened steps, refused to be hurried. Dempsey had not known such joy since he had been sanctified or saved in the little log church on Bear Creek. He broke into song, and his deep voice cascaded through the empty summer woods.

There was always a contradiction about the Methodist church on the frontier. Organized as an episcopal rather than a congregational church, the bishops appointed itinerant preachers. The contradiction is that the somewhat undemocratic Methodists served the democratic frontier well. The bishops were like army generals sending their roving scouts to penetrate the vast frontier. The circuit rider and the Methodist doctrine of free grace won a large and steady response in the mountains.

Dempsey, Grant's father, came into the ministry of The Methodist Episcopal Church North and worked for its establishment in Kentucky against heavy religious and political odds. The slavery question, the Civil War, and the fracture of the Methodist Church over slavery in 1844 had left a residue of hate and bitterness even in the church. From its beginning in America the church of its Anglican founder, John Wesley, had firmly opposed slavery.

Before 1844 the church laws on slavery were strict. Members who owned slaves had to obey the decision of their local church as to when to sell them. They were also expected to free their slaves if the laws of their state permitted. Church officials could not own slaves.

In 1844 it was the last prohibition which had triggered the secession of the southern churches to form The Methodist Church South. The wife of Bishop Andrews had inherited slaves. Bishop Andrews himself had bought no slaves, but under an archaic law, now discarded, he was considered to be the owner of all property of his wife. He promptly gave up his rights to his wife's property and could legally claim that he owned no slaves.

But by this time the growing emotions about the morality of slavery itself had become more important than the legalisms of the church and common law. The Methodist Church divided bitterly, not to join hands again until 1938.

This early secession was feared by Kentucky Congressman Henry Clay. He wrote to a friend: "Scarcely any public occurrence has gaven me so much real concern. I would not say that it would necessarily produce a dissolution of the political union of these states, but the example would be fraught with imminent danger."[7]

That night by candle light Dempsey and Elizabeth looked at the map of his circuit. He would be eighty miles from home, enormous distances to Elizabeth who had never been more than fifteen miles from home. Even with an automobile and good roads, it would have been a big assignment. Dempsey had only his horse and the mountain trails. Elizabeth was happy and proud of him, willing to accept her burden of caring for the farm and three small sons during his long absences. Dempsey was exultant. He was going to do God's work.

According to the rules of the church then, he was not accepted without conditions. His almost total lack of any formal education was no obstacle. The mountain preachers were homespun theologians, deriving their authority directly from God and their mountain neighbors.

Dempsey had a rich deep voice, or a "degree of utterance." He would later be locally well-known as the Moody of the mountains, after the famous nineteenth century evangelist, Dwight L. Moody.

Rules of the church for his conduct were detailed and strict. He was to be punctual and was to believe evil in no one unless he saw it done. The Commandment against false gossip was more carefully observed then. He was to rise at 4:00 A.M. to read scriptures with notes, and was "to read the most useful books and that regularly and constantly." He was told "to develop a taste for reading or return to his former employment."[8] Illiteracy was not a part of the Methodist doctrine.

He was forbidden to use alcohol or tobacco and was "to extirpate from the Church those who sold goods and have not paid the duty on them by the government." This had a sharp and definite meaning in the mountains, for moonshine whiskey was that on which no excise tax was paid. He was warned that the devil was real and "travels no ground but, like a stinking fog, leaves a scent behind."[9]

He began his work almost at once, packing his Bible, Methodist Discipline, Hymnal, and a few personal belongings into two saddle bags. He was away most of the year of 1870, sometimes during harvest time, riding all night to get home just to go to work in the fields without sleeping.

In 1871 he was appointed to the Williamsburg Circuit, closer to home. Elizabeth could now see how gaunt and tired he was becoming. Exposure to wind, rain, and snow, and his own intense devotion, were taking their toll. He was reappointed in 1872, but church records then fall silent, not even noting his death in 1875, of tuberculosis, at the ripe age of 36.

Many circuit preachers died young, but not all. Brother Scales, a Scottish minister from Virginia, probably visited Dempsey and Elizabeth on Meadowcreek. But he is recorded as having visited Elizabeth's sister, Samantha Faulkner on Jack's Fork a few miles away. There, in the cracking cold one winter morning he was offered a kettle of warm water. "But he waved it away: and taking two towels, marched off to the frozen branch. He broke the ice with the heel of his boot, pulled off his shirt, and scrubbed his face, neck, and waist." In the zero weather he rubbed himself dry with the other towel. He was at that time 70.[10]

When one adds to this hard life the feuds born of the Civil War and of the moonshining wars and the growing number of first timber and then coal camps, it is not surprising that in the middle nineteenth century the murder rate in some mountain counties made New York City look like a haven of law and order.

Lively former Circuit Judge Jennings Bryan Johnson, as a young district attorney, remembered trying thirteen murder cases in one three month term of court. But there was a surprising reason for the later decline in the murder rate.

Before there were adequate roads, the men in the growing number of coal camps could not escape on weekends. A minor slight or curse heard through the fog of corn whiskey would usually erupt into gunfire, for everyone went armed. Later, when better roads allowed the miners to go home, the murder rate went down substantially.

But, because of the strong tradition of religion there, Judge Johnson remembers that few murders ever happened on Meadowcreek. Dempsey and the other ministers who often made the cabin of Buck Perkins, Dempsey's father, their gathering place, must have done their work well.

As do the trees in the woods where he now lies, Dempsey sweetened the earth around him. The mountain church of which he was a small part brought a light into the rough mountains which helped Grant, Dempsey's son, escape the illiteracy and the violence of his time and place.[11]

2. Dempsey White Perkins
the Circuit Rider
about 1870

3. Elizabeth Sharp Perkins
his wife

(From a tin type reproduced by Fox Studio, Carrollton, Ohio)

Chapter Four
Life In A Log Cabin

In the 1870's the cabin that Dempsey had built in 1860 was weathered and smoke-blackened. A porch had been added along one side and in the back a lean-to with two small rooms. A ladder poked through the ceiling to an upstairs loft where six boys slept on straw mattresses.

All the cooking was done in the big stone fireplace which dominated the main room. The family never owned a cook stove. Sometimes in winter, old newspapers were plastered on the coldest wall for insulation. Especially in winter, cutting wood was a daily chore. So the axe and the saw were vital tools of survival. Their importance can be reflected in their sale prices. In 1824 Solomon Perkin's things were sold after his death. An axe brought $1.25 and a saw $5.43, but a cow only $4.50.

Even baking was done in the fireplace in a deep iron skillet known as a dutch oven. Fitted with a heavy lid, it was buried deep in the coals so that the loaf would bake evenly. A rock ledge sheltered the spring near the cabin. The spring and Cotton Creek, a branch of Meadowcrook, were the only running water Grant ever knew.

In the mountains there was a strong prejudice against pumps. Water had to be exposed to air. If it stood overnight, it was dead water, not good to drink. Washing clothes was done by the side of the creek, where a crude stone furnace heated water in an iron kettle. Soap was made with two plentiful by-products of the farm — hog fat and wood ashes.

The progeny of hogs and chickens was a perpetual supply of meat and eggs. A large garden, surrounded by a strong picket fence to keep out marauders, was always plowed and fertilized with manure from the barn in the fall. In spring it began to produce onions, potatoes, bunch beans, pole beans, beets, tomatoes, cabbages, and even cotton. Seed was saved from the year before.

Corn was the main field crop, for it had more than one use — as corn meal and whiskey. A gritter hung on the wall to grate the corn for roasting ear bread. Whiskey was not only pleasant drink but also, in the mountains, an economic necessity. The corn and grain that could not be easily stored or moved to market could be made into an imperishable and valuable product, corn whiskey, often used as money. In 1816 in another part of Kentucky, Tom Lincoln had traded his farm for $20.00 in cash and "ten bar'ls" of whiskey. Then he took his family a hundred miles to Indiana. His whiskey was money in the bank to buy a farm there.[12]

But Dempsey did not have to take his corn very far. His father "Buck" was well known for his good whiskey. He was what an old man once called a "Govamint distiller", meaning he paid his federal excise taxes. He also made whiskey under contract with the Union Army, a fact well-known to Confederate raiding parties in nearby Tennessee who often lifted his current batch for themselves. In the mountains whiskey was a medicine, a sealer of bargains and farm trades. It warmed one in the winter and cooled one in summer.

Grant owned a long-barreled muzzle-loading rifle. As a boy and later as a soldier he was an excellent shot. When his mother wanted a chicken for supper, he would shoot it in the head as it strutted unsuspectingly around the farm yard. He could pick a squirrel out of the top of a tree.[13]

Grant also fished the clear creeks and trapped for possum, mink, and muskrat. Seventy-five cents for a mink skin was to him a small fortune. One would command fifty dollars now. He worked in the garden, in the fields ploughing and cutting briars, and in the forest cutting wood and logging.

It was a life of hard labor, but it would be a mistake to think of it only as back-breaking and unrewarding. He lived in a compact and stable society bounded by the hills of his valley and surrounded by his own kinfolk.

Then, mountain life was so slow moving and unchanging as

to appear timeless and eternal.

Neither life, language, nor ways had changed much since Grant's great-great-grandfather Solomon had built his cabin in the virgin forest of Meadowcreek Valley in 1814. Life had a continuity of land and kinfolk, especially one's own kin or the tribe. One's kinfolk took care of the elderly, the sick, and the orphaned children. They were the only welfare department.

When Dempsey coughed out his last bit of life in 1875, his father "Buck" and his uncle Timothy gave 50 acres of their land to Elizabeth, so that she could raise her six small boys. To help her, when the fields had to be worked, were many of Grant's uncles and cousins. Elizabeth did not allow her sons to be parcelled out among the other cabins.

Grant's family on Meadowcreek had used the land, water, and animals without dominating or destroying them. The roadless forest, the tangled canebrake, and the steep hills had imposed their own apparently eternal limitations. A crop grown, soap made, an acre cleared of the massive stumps of the climax hardwoods, a road hacked from the brush, were tiny victories of an emerging society.

Grant's people would be astonished today that man could now change mountains, and turn rivers. And even more astonished that men, by doing so, could believe they could free themselves from the natural limitations of the earth.

Their lives were also deeply lonely. That was why "gatherin's" of all kind were important. Even church camp meetings were as much social events as religious. Mountain hospitality was real. Such invitations as: "I'm sure mighty proud to have you heppin aroun". Or "Don't go hurren away. Keep a settin." were meant to be accepted.

When Grant was seven, Kentucky had the meagre beginnings of a public education, a log school three miles from his home where school was held three months in the year. Because books were scarce, it was a "blab" school, using oral recitation. Even so, his generation was almost the first to have any public education at all in Meadowcreek Valley.

Even though illiteracy in the mountains was three times that of the rest of the country, mountain people were not unintelligent. Written tests and measurements, of all kinds —

I.Q., civil service, college entrance, psychological, aptitude — to which we are now addicted, are often not the real tests of ability.

John C. Campbell gave us the same message about the mountain people in 1921. "If we accept as a definition of education, adaptation of life to the environment, many a Highlander would compare favorably with some of the college graduates who have come into the community to educate him."[14]

Then there was the boredom, as well as the excitement, of the Methodist meeting house nearby. Boredom, because a boy must sit through hours of sermons. Excitement because religious emotion often swept the congregation in a primitive sanctuary which nevertheless often evoked the very presence of God.

But religion was not the only commodity brought into the mountain meeting houses. There was the intellectual ferment of news from the outside brought by the circuit riding preachers. In the mountains, the Methodist Church was not a quiet cloister and its mountain preachers were not monks. They were in the thick of things among the people.

Finally, in a time when, in the mountains, there were no libraries, few books, and almost no newspapers, Grant once wrote that he was raised on *The Youth's Companion* and read the entire issue the day it arrived.[15]

Chapter Five
The Youth's Companion

One never quite knows what tiny spark may fire a young mind to want to know more, to read and to think, to compare and contrast, to stretch the mind into the unknown, to feel the waking up of intellectual passion.

Grant could easily have lived out his life as a mountain farmer, satisfied to raise a few hogs, to put out a few acres of corn and potatoes, to hunt deer, and to warm himself with whiskey in the winter. There was little stimulus to do much else.

Intellectual intensity is hinted at in the fact that he read the entire issue of the *Companion* the day it arrived.[16] What in those closed packed pages interested this mountain boy of fourteen in 1886 and 1887? Published by the Perry Mason Company of Boston, it was a ten or twelve page weekly tabloid, costing $1.75 a year. Since Grant's mother probably never had an income of more than $50.00 a year, this was not a cheap magazine.

The young are now surrounded by intellectual stimuli of all kinds, but Grant only heard the sounds and silences of the forest. The Bible, some Methodist material, an occasional newspaper, and a few school books were the only reading materials other than *The Youth's Companion* to come into Elizabeth Perkins' home.

Each issue of the *Companion* included a serial story, a children's page, and articles on current events, science, and travel in foreign lands. Most of the stories were by new authors who competed for annual prizes up to $5000. These very generous prizes brought thousands of responses from budding authors. But there were also famous authors such as William Dean Howells and Edward Everett Hale.

The editors proudly announced a coming article by Prof. T.H. Huxley called "From Hut to Pantheon", explaining evolution. The *Companion* wasn't afraid to tackle controversial subjects.

The international and historical scope of the articles in the *Companion* in 1886 is surprising. There were articles about China, Abyssinia (Ethiopia), France, India, Egypt, Tripoli, Alaska, Italy, and Canada. One learned that China makes no provision for the poor but, instead, recognizes the profession of begging. "Thus, if a crowd of fifty to one hundred creatures, so filthy and diseased as to be hardly recognized as human beings, should besiege the doors of a store in Peking and refuse to move until their demands for money had been met, it would be no use for the merchant to appeal to the police. They would be answered: 'Well, give them what they want. It isn't much and they will then go away.' It is not strange that under such a system beggars thrive and grow fat." (December 23, 1886)

The Nineteenth century was just as preoccupied with Russia as is the Twentieth century. There were more articles about that country than about any other, some of which, in 1887, foretold the events of 1917. There was a story about a demonstration of students in St. Petersburg. "It was a striking feature of this affair that among the students were over a hundred young women who belonged to the medical classes at the university."

In 1887 there were certainly not hundreds of women in medical schools in America, a surprising insight into Russia during the last century. Nor would the *Companion* have approved. Even an article about the growing demand and good pay for shorthand reporters (March 31, 1887) was told in the male gender, without even an invitation to the girls to try this promising new profession.

About the empire of the Czar (April 7, 1887): "So vast in its extent that it bewilders the mind to attempt to form a picture of it. To the people of the narrowed kingdoms of Europe, who watch jealously every movement of Russia, the empire is mysterious and fearful. It is no wonder that the statesmen of Europe have Russia seldom out of mind and sometimes attribute to her the strangest and darkest purposes, some of them most unlikely for her to entertain." That sentence could have been written in 1984 as well as in 1887.

Readers were told about the Russian nihilist conspirators. "The recent desperate attempt upon the life of the Russian Czar, which took place on or near the very spot on the Newsky Prospect where his father was murdered six years ago shows that the desperate spirit which prompted that act still survives." (April 21, 1887)

The nihilists were often from the upper classes, military officers, and university students. "This is a striking feature of the Russian revolutionary movement. In most countries, conspirators against the state have been unlearned and, usually, poor men who have nothing to lose from anarchy. But in Russia the nihilists seem to belong altogether to the upper and middle classes."

The article ended with the following editorial comment. "This is the penalty that the Czar has to pay for the absoluteness of his rule. Political freedom affords a safety valve for the utterance of disaffection. So long as the Czar remains a despot, some sort of secret and dangerous combination will continue to exist."

Finally, there was a story proving that the Soviets did not begin the Russian secret police. In 1863 a Frenchman, after visiting Russia, wrote a book with some "stringent comments on the conditions of the lower classes." The book was banned in Russia and never even widely read in France. Twenty years later, in 1883, the author's brother was visiting Russia.

On his arrival at the border he was visited by the police who asked him if he was the kinsman of the author of the banned book. He was escorted to the noon train to Meml outside Russia. "It was useless to resist", wrote the unlucky traveler. "He accompanied me to the train and sat beside me. At Meml, he took leave of me. 'Monsieur is now outside Russia. A mere hint is sufficient to a person of his intelligence.'"

Health was a popular subject in the *Companion*. There were articles explaining the causes, symptoms, and cures for speech derangement, "washerwoman's hands" (arthritis), granulated eyelids, fits of sneezing, the wonders of surgery because of anesthetics, lock jaw (its cause unknown), and even dandruff. Sound familiar?

The cocaine habit was the subject of an article in March 1887, telling of an experiment that a doctor performed on himself. "The next night he injected two grains, and the same pleasant feeling followed, accompanied by an inordinate desire to write. He thought at the time that his work was the best that he had ever done, but found it in the morning, to be disconnected nonsense, each sentence having no relation to another."

One issue announced prizes up to $1000 for new subscriptions. Also a mouth-watering list of premiums that you could get with one new subscription and a few cents. What delights they must have seemed to a fourteen year old mountain boy.

Pictured in enticing detail were pens, ice skates, footballs, fishing rods, magic lanterns, pocket knives, chemistry sets, clockwork locomotives, violins, cornets, mandolins, guitars, watches, sewing machines, carpet sweepers, cameras, woodworking lathes, dolls, doll dishes, toy steam engines, and a brass toy steamboat (one subscription and ten cents). Even though Grant had never seen most of these marvelous objects, *The Youth's Companion* showed him the world outside his isolated home valley.

His mother had seen that Grant was not as wild and as boisterous as many mountain boys. Grant's older brother Joe also sensed this. Once, when he and Grant were working in the fields, Joe, then fourteen, told his eight year old brother that Grant should get an education. That was unusual in a fourteen year old boy anywhere and anytime.

Many people can look back on their childhood and youth to a book, a favorite uncle or aunt, or even to a favorite place where the intellect awakened and where they had an urge to know more and to read more.

When I was growing up, Grant's untidy study was a place of fascination to me. Most of the time he served small churches that did not provide a study in the church. It was at home. When he was preparing a sermon, the door was closed and we had to be quiet. Otherwise, his children could help themselves to its cluttered contents.

A mounted deerhead was on the wall, its antlers useful for hanging up hats and scarves, a trophy from a hunt. His sword as a captain in the Kentucky Volunteer Cavalry in the Spanish American war hung on the wall. Its long bright curved blade was etched with his name and rank. It was only a ceremonial sword and couldn't cut a piece of cheese.

His diplomas, in imposing Latin, were hung on the wall. His typewriter was of ancient design, its letter keys poised high above the page and ready to pounce. A long wooden box was the filing cabinet for his sermons.

A battered rolltop desk had many nooks and drawers, one being filled with coins he had brought back from his travels — Turkish, Egyptian, Italian, Greek, and German. There was also a red Turkish fez useful as a head covering at home.

But his books interested me more than anything else. I was always looking curiously into them. There were books about religion, which I did not understand, magazines, The Harvard Classics, and novels. But I remember best Stoddards *Illustrated Travels,* filled with pictures, in many volumes. I spent hours reading them.

Stoddard's lectures sparked in me a lifelong interest in history and the conviction that if you want your children to read, fill your house with books. They will find some of them.

The Youth's Companion was just such a catalyst for Grant; and gave him as good an understanding of the outside world as any television program or textbook does today. To an imaginative boy with a mind wide-awake, who had never seen a railroad locomotive, an electric light, a flush toilet, a river passenger steamer, a typewriter, or a library of books, who had never heard another language or dialect spoken, the intellectual excitement of *The Youth's Companion* must have been volcanic; and very early sparked in him a desire to get out of the isolated valleys of his homeland into the world.

Chapter Six
A Photograph of 1886

To Edgar Allen Poe, the mountain people were an uncouth race. They were rough, yes. But even though they had been left in the backwaters of the swift and broad American river, they did have an efficient civilization within the American commonwealth. The people described in the previous pages lived and loved, worked and played, despaired and exulted, and had their ups and downs. They were real people, not caricatures.

And finally, they were discovered by the eastern literary magazines. In the summer of 1886 James Lane Allen rode through Whitley County from Burnside, where the railroad ended, on his way to the Cumberland Gap. He could likely have come down Meadowcreek Valley. He wrote of this trip in *Harper's New Monthly Magazine* in a piece called *Through the Cumberland Gap on Horseback.*[17]

"It is but a short distance from the blue grass country to the eastern mountains; but in traversing it you detach yourself from all that you have experienced, and take up the history of the English speaking men and women at a point a hundred or a hundred fifty years ago."

Burnside was the transition point between the elegant blue grass region of Kentucky and the primitive world Allen was about to enter. A fruit stand at the railroad station had bananas. A mountain man, seeing bananas for the first time, said: "Blame me if them ain't the darndest beans I ever seen."

The subject of a coon dog started a conversation, just as it will today in rural America: "Were there many coons in the woods?" "There were several." "Several" in the mountain dictionary meant a great number. "Do coons eat corn?" "Coons is as bad as hogs on corn when they get tuk to it."

Allen described the wild tangle of a climax forest that represents the final triumph of the giant hardwoods over the lesser trees. "Meanwhile, the darkness was falling and the scenery along the road grew wilder and grander. On the summits were the tanbark oaks, lower down the white oaks, and lower yet the fine specimens of yellow poplar. From the valleys to the crests a dense underbrush, save where the ground has been burnt over year after year to improve grazing."

The roads were either non-existant or only traces. "I say route because there wasn't always a road, and but for the guide there would not always be a direction. Here the wild calacanthus blooms and fills the air with fragrance and the white camellia throws open its white and purple splendors."

Allen described the people with stark candor but without human depth. Grant as a boy and his grandfather Buck and uncles and cousins must have looked to astonished outsiders as the mountain people appeared to wide-eyed James Allen. The people were: "straight, slim, angular, without great muscular robustness, features regular and colorless, unanimated but intelligent, in the men sometimes fierce and in the women sometimes sad."

"A manner shy and deferential but kind and fearless; eyes with a long slow look of inquiry, or of general listlessness; the key to life a low minor strain; losing itself in reveries, voices monotonous; living today as their ancestors did a hundred years ago; hearing nothing of the world and caring nothing for it: responding feebly to the influences of civilization."

About the land, which most owned or claimed to own: "The great body of the people live on and cultivate patches which they either own or hold free. These [people] not infrequently get together and trade farms as they would horses, no deeds being exchanged. Most are abjectly poor and they appear to have no sense of accumulation. In some regions the great problem in life is to raise two dollars a year for county taxes." Then there was illicit or non-taxed whiskey. Its manufacture "is a considerable source of revenue, and a desperate self-destructive sub source of revenue from the same business — the betrayal of its hidden sources. There is no thing harder or more dangerous to find in the mountains than a hidden still."

He also told of a former important source of money for mountain people — the herb "sang" or ginseng. Its digging was a general occupation, for which China was an important market. Allen wrote: "It has nearly all been dug out except in the wildest parts of the country where entire families may be seen out 'sanging'. . . . They took it to town in bags, selling it for a dollar and a half a pound. This was mainly the labor of women and children who went to work barefooted amid briars, chestnut burrs, copperhead and rattlesnakes. . . . A few years ago, one of the counties was nearly depopulated in consequence of a great exodus into Arkansas whence had come the news that 'sang' was plentiful."

Other wild herbs gathered were appleroots, ginger, golden seal, and blood root. The mountaineer's principal drink was coffee, "bitter and black, not having been roasted but burnt." Mountain teas were made from golden rod and wintergreen which "they mollify with homemade sorghum molasses which they call 'long sweetening' or with sugar which they call 'short sweetening'." Allen described the feuds. "The special origins of these are various; the blood heated and tempers lost under the influence of moonshining; reporting on the places of manufacture; local politics; survival of resentments engendered by the Civil War."

Of their hospitality: "But while thus cruel and bitter toward each other, they present to strangers the aspect of a polite, kind, and most hospitable race. They will divide with you shelter and warmth and food however scant; and will put themselves to trouble for your convenience with an unreckoning earnest friendliness and good nature that is touching to the last degree."

"Buck", my father's grandfather, a mountain patriarch of 69, died in May 1886 among his four hundred acres. James Allen had described the abject poverty and the miserable cultivated patches he saw everywhere in the mountains that year. Buck must have been more prosperous than most.

Chapter Seven
Appearance In A Garden

Elizabeth Perkins looked out the door of her cabin in time to see the sun dip behind the hill across the creek. Sunset always came early and quickly in the valleys. It was early spring of 1889. Two of her sons, William and Joe, were on the sloped field, spreading manure and cutting briars in preparation for spring planting. Her youngest son Grant, a long-boned boy of fifteen, appeared around the corner of the barn with a hat full of eggs.

"Put the eggs in the crock and call the others," she said. "It's most supper time." The big room was warm and smelled of supper cooking. Grant ran across the big squared log that served as a foot bridge across the creek, and up the slope of the long hill.

Elizabeth watched him a moment and turned slowly back into the log farm house to continue with the preparation of supper. The black iron kettle steamed over the glowing logs in the big open fireplace, and filled the house with the rich scent of salt pork and beans.

The unpainted puncheon floor was clean but bare. Pegged wooden benches flanked the big oak table. There was a small rocking chair, two massive chests, and a side table with pots, pans, and other simple household goods of the times. Three long-barreled muzzle-loading rifles stood in their niches in the wall.

Since the death of her husband Dempsey fourteen years earlier, she had kept her family together; and by hard and incessant work, had given food, shelter, and spirit to sustain her six boys. She had a gentle, serious face and still dark brown hair, tied in a bun.

Her nephew, James B. Faulkner, her sister Samantha's boy, once visited his cousin Grant. He wrote: "Grant was near my age but younger, but I was no match for him in size and strength. His family, like mine, had undergone many hardships. But his mother had been able to keep her home, and it seemed to me that they were in better circumstances than my father, Frank Faulkner. She made an indelible impression on me as a woman of character, gentleness, patience, and kindness. Her manner of speaking was very quiet and appealing."[18]

Elizabeth watched from the cabin door as the springless wagon came rocking down the steep hill, pushing the grey mules ahead of it. They splashed across the ford in the creek. Bill jumped boisterously off the wagon before it stopped. Joe, always the more serious of the boys, took charge of the mules. With Grant's help he unhitched them, put them in their stalls, and gave them a basket of oats. The boys washed up on the long porch and entered the twilight-filled cabin with shouts and horseplay.

Their talk died down as Elizabeth bent her head for evening prayer. There was only her voice and the sound of the fire. The loud talk was not resumed. When the strangely quiet meal was finished, Elizabeth, old at fifty from the hard life, spoke with an effort to her sons.

"You've been good boys to me. Strong hands, like your Pa's before he took sick and died of the consumption. Grant and George never really knew him. But God spoke in him." She paused, her face showing strong signs of things unseen. No one spoke until she spoke again.

"But I saw him last night. Like a dream. His face was white and thin like it was when he died. He beckoned me, but when I looked up again he was gone."

She looked with pity on her sons, now silent in the dim twilight of the cabin. There was no disbelief present, for visions were a real part of religious life in the mountains.

"He beckoned me, boys, and I must go. I won't be with you after a spell." She fell silent and let her work worn hands fall into her lap. Strength drained from her as though she was already surrendering her life to her God.

Grant lay that night on his straw mattress in the loft without sleeping. His mother had been a source of security and comfort to him. Now he was frightened.

To the young, death is an unreal apparition. In the private darkness, tears came, and he dug his fingers desperately into the straw ticking. Moonlight drifted silently through the small windows. He could hear the contented sounds of birds nesting in the chinks between the logs.

An overpowering sense of the mystery of God came over him. His dead father had appeared to his mother and she was to die. The mind, being mortal, could not understand this; but the soul, being immortal, could.

Sleep finally came to a day he never forgot. Less than a year later Elizabeth was buried beside her husband Dempsey on the hill overlooking their home. Grant told me, his oldest son, this story over fifty years ago when he and I were alone one Sunday afternoon at home. I can remember the feeling of truth that overpowered my youthful skepticism.

Grant once wrote about the night of her death. "She was motionless and white. She wanted to talk to me. In broken voice and words often indistinct she asked me to take up the work of my father. In the years that followed, I tried to escape that commission but could not."

Chapter Eight

Army Volunteer

After the death of his mother, Grant lived and worked on the farms of his older brothers Joe and Felix, as a restless sojourner. As kinfolk he was welcome, but he felt he had no real place. Between the ages of sixteen and nineteen he did chores, plowed, cleared new land and hauled tanbark logs out of the forest.

He missed his brother George very much. As the two youngest, they had been good friends, had hunted, fished, and trapped together, and had told each other about their dreams and plans. But in 1889 after their mother's death, George, at the age of 18, had gone to the newest state of Washington. Joe, by now the family's steady patriarch even at the age of 24, had helped George with train fare on the Northern Pacific. As the last of the land grant railroads, it had completed the northern line a few years earlier. But now Joe recognized the irritable unease of his strong-willed younger brother.

Even in 1892 the West was still the great beneficial safety valve that allowed penniless young men to escape poverty. George homesteaded land near Rosalia, Washington, and wrote Grant about the immense green forests and mountains of eastern Washington and of the plentiful deer and bear. George never returned east. Until his death in 1936 George remained essentially a frontier hunter all his life. His sons only persuaded him to quit carrying a forty-five revolver late in life.

At nineteen, Grant was over six feet tall and a hard-bodied 170 pounds. Maybe one of George's infrequent letters spurred him to follow George to Washington. His plan was to work the wheat harvests north to earn enough for a cheap train ticket on the Northern Pacific. In those days it was possible to work all summer with the wheat-threshing crews as they progressed northward.

In the summer of 1892 Grant and Joe drove to the train station at Williamsburg behind two work-worn mules. Joe was sad that his little brother was going. Perhaps both of them remembered what their mother had wished on her death bed — that Grant would take up his father's work as a minister.

But in a blaze of excitement about going west, Grant was youthfully careless of such dying wishes.

At the station, the train bound north came slowly past them. Its round nose topped by a large square head lamp, its bell loudly proclaiming, the train spouted steam, smoke, and incredible excitement. As the tall drive wheels came to a stop, heads appeared at the open windows of the two wooden passenger cars.

The station erupted into chaotic activity. Men in the baggage and freight cars and on the platform put on or took off crates of squawking chickens, hogs, heifers, lumber, bales of tanbark, trunks, freight packing cases, and leather pouches of mail.

The station platform was full of people, many not going anywhere but wishing they were. The trains had only come to Williamsburg seven years earlier. Grant and his brothers had sometimes ridden in to see this new wonder of the world. To all boys in the railroad age, trains were wonderful visitors from far away places. Their destinations were always alabaster cities.

Grant boarded the open platform of the passenger car, a cheap carpet bag holding all his simple possessions. The activity in the station, which had only looked chaotic, suddenly subsided into a calm expectancy. Everyone waited the signal of the blue uniformed conductor. He stood studying a big gold watch, aware of the part in the little drama that he played. Finally, with a dramatic flourish signaling a high ball (full speed ahead) in a voice worthy of the Metropolitan Opera, he announced that all were to get aboard.

Joe and Grant exchanged a few awkward words of goodbye, which hid their true feelings. As the train moved out of the station, Grant looked back at his brother, the little town, and the hills that had been his home, suddenly a little scared and sorry he was going. But only for a moment. The train carried him from one moment of expectation to another: towns and cities he had heard of and read about but had never seen, Corbin, London, and Lexington, Kentucky, the blue grass plains with their handsome white houses, Louisville and the wide Ohio River with its huge passenger steamers.

By stages he reached Chicago, the booming, brawny, fastest growing city in America, the nerve center for a vast railroad system. In Carl Sandburg's words, "the hog butcher of the world". A giant industrial center, it was also alive with debating clubs and intellectual ferment. In 1892 the famous lawyer Clarence Darrow was there, reading poetry at the Sunset Club, debating economics at the Henry George Club, and helping Peter Atgeld get elected Governor.[19]

In 1892 Darrow was general counsel for the Chicago and Northwestern Railroad, a job from which he would resign in 1894 to defend the labor leader Eugene Debs in a criminal charge following the tumultuous Pullman strike. Today, that would be like quitting as General Motors' lawyer to defend a communist.

But to Grant, the nineteen-year old boy from the mountains, Chicago was the clamor of hundreds of wagons, their iron tires clanging on the stone streets, an endless stream of people, confusing heaps of buildings, and hundreds of ships and schooners on Lake Michigan. It was an exhilarating mix of sounds and sights.

In June, 1892, Grant was in a cheap hotel room in St. Paul, Minnesota, with still not enough money for a ticket to the State of Washington. In the depression of that year he could find no work. He was homesick and lonely, but he found some friends in the pool room at the hotel, one of them an army recruiting sergeant.

Where did this minister-to-be learn to play pool? He always liked sports. But he probably would never have gone into that pool hall in St. Paul if he had not known the game. At nineteen, young males simply did not admit to their peers that they were lacking such young male accomplishments.

Undoubtedly, when he and his brothers had sometimes gone to Williamsburg, they had stopped to play pool.

Grant once wrote that he was forced into the army by hard times. His pool hall recruiter friend persuaded him to join, maybe painting a glowing picture of army life. The enlistment was duly recorded in the archaic hand of a long-forgotten War Department clerk in the Register of Enlistments: "Ulysses S. G. Perkins, July 22, 1892. Enlisted at St. Paul, Minn., by Captain Wilhelm for five years. Born Whitley County, Ky., age 21 years 4 months. Occupation: laborer. Ht. 6 foot 7/8., Wt. 170 lbs."

So he lied about his age. But maybe Captain Wilhelm knew he was only nineteen and discreetly added two more years to help his quota of enlistments. It was, after all, an all volunteer army. In those fine and free days, you did not carry a birth certificate, driver's license, draft registration, social security card, bail bond undertaking, or credit cards. The computer had not yet reduced his humanity to a series of numbers. When you said who you were, you were believed for your own sake.[20]

4. Private Ulysses S. G. Perkins
12th U.S. Infantry, Fort Sully, South Dakota, 1892
(Photo by R. L. Kelly, Pierre, S. D.)

PROPERTY OF
SEYBERT U. M. CHURCH

Chapter Nine
Fort Sully, South Dakota

In 1892, the U.S. Army totalled only about 26,000 men, scattered mostly in small forts in the west to keep an eye on the Indians. Perched on a bluff on the Missouri River about 25 miles north of Pierre, Fort Sully was typical.

On the train from St. Paul, Grant saw the dark fir forests and lakes of Minnesota thin out into the empty plains of South Dakota, unlike anything he had ever seen. In the narrow valleys of Kentucky he had rarely seen sunsets or sunrises. Now, as the train rolled deeper into the once undisputed land of The Sioux, the horizon stretched out endlessly in all directions, and the sky was luminous in its prairie brilliance.

The rails seemed to unwind under him. He looked for small signs of life, a small herd of buffalo, the lonely sod house of a settler, a band of small deer, a horseman on a small hill (maybe an Indian). He was having some regrets. He would now never get to Washington. Maybe Joe would have sent him the money to go home, but he was determined to be on his own. Anyhow, It was too late. He did feel some excitement going into Indian country.

Arriving at the raw two year old capitol of Pierre, he went down to the river where he stood in the clutter and grime of freight, livestock, new settlers, and Indians on a tough little Missouri River steamboat for the 25 mile trip to Fort Sully. At the Fort's dock, he apprehensively walked across the huge dusty parade ground to the command post, and stiffly announced to Major J. H. Gageby that he was reporting for duty.[21]

If he had expected an exciting life as a frontier soldier, he was at once introduced to an unexpected enemy — boredom. The last and strangest of the Indian troubles had happened in 1890 and 1891 with Wounded Knee and the Ghost Dance troubles, and the peace of despair and exhaustion of the Indians had finally come. So Grant had missed all the action, although he did not know it that day in July, 1892.[22]

Since there was really nothing for them to do of any importance, garrison duty became a deadly and boring routine. The soldiers gathered the enormous quantities of wood required to keep them warm in the bitter Dakota winters. They harvested hay for the horses and the stock, made adobe bricks for repair of the buildings, and drilled on the parade ground. Earlier, when the railroad and telegraph lines were being built, they had marched out to protect the work crews. But that work was now finished. So, for month after month, all the commander had to report to his superiors was: "Garrison performed routine duties." These forts were already obsolete in 1892.

The Fort canteen and the saloons at Pierre were almost the only recreation for the soldiers. Inevitably, alcohol and drunkenness became a problem in the army then. Grant often saw the following scene. "Soldiers paid off, times very lively in the camp, especially around the canteen where the beer flowed freely. The ground completely covered by empty bottles. Fights in all parts of the camp."[23]

The arrival of a regimental band was a welcome event in the autumn of 1893. The last time such music had been heard at Fort Sully had been an 1885 when an Italian bandmaster had played a farewell concert, performing two pieces of his own composition. He had been Achille LaGuardia, whose son Fiorella would become the famous and flamboyant mayor of New York City in the 1930's.

But the big news at Fort Sully in 1894 was its abandonment as no longer needed. The Indians had finally been pacified — mostly by disease, degradation, hopelessness, and broken promises. With the disappearance of the buffalo, perhaps their fate was inevitable. So the order came in September, 1894, for the 12th Infantry to go to Fort Niobrara (Swift River to the Sioux) near Valentine in northwestern Nebraska, leaving a band of 20 soldiers to guard Fort Sully's sixty-three empty buildings on the empty plains.

The day the 12th Infantry left Fort Sully was the most exciting Grant had seen. The Pierre *Free Press* described the soldiers as "a gentlemanly lot ... overflowing with generosity born of making brighter the conditions of their fellow men."[24] One is skeptical of that glowing description when one notes that the Surgeon General's report for 1894 said that alcoholism at Fort Sully was more prevalant than at other forts.

The editor then got carried away. "The battalion marched down from the Fort Saturday, but it was not until the next morning that packing was completed. At departure a rousing cheer went up. A fluttering of cambric filled the air with a sweet odor as the manly boys in blue were lost from sight." The troop train was made up of several freight cars, three coaches for the soldiers, and a palace sleeping car for the officers.

Grant felt like a hero even though, in two years, he had only waged battle against the mosquito, the barrack's rats, and flies so thick he often had to strain them out of his coffee before he could drink it.

He wrote about those days while in New York in 1905, a piece called *Army Life In The Great Northwest* No. 17, *How Captain McGowan Took the Camp.* He must have written other stories of the army but only one manuscript was ever found.

"In the early nineties the 12th Infantry was stationed in the wilds of South Dakota. The dreary landscape, the everlasting weird rustle of the wind, the howl of a coyote, and an occasional sight of sly, revengeful Sioux, were about the only things of interest to the tired doughboys whose monotonous garrison duty was quite out of keeping with the stories of the wild and woolly west. The hours were longest during winter when all exercises were in quarters, or during the summer when the intense heat made drills and battle maneuvers impossible.

"But autumn days brought the annual practice marches and sham battles that were always welcomed by the soldier. Then was the tent life, the relaxation from garrison duty, the exhilaration of rapid marches and of short decisive battles.

"September, the most glorious month of the great northwest, had come, and a company of the 'dirty dozen' was in the field commanded by Major Gageby. After a hard day's march, the command had reached the banks of the Missouri, at a place not far from the camp of Sitting Bull in 1876 before he was driven across the Missouri and before the tragic Little Bighorn. The boys were too tired for camp frolics that night.

"Early the next morning, it was learned that Captain McGowan had taken a few picked men and with these declared that he would take the camp. At camp, guards were doubled, and pickets thrown well out to watch for the approach of the enemy. About 10:30 rifle shots were heard to the northeast, and the approach of the enemy was reported by mounted scouts.

"Assembly was sounded, and the sleepy camp was immediately turned into hustle and bustle. The columns started moving toward the scene of the shots. Pickets falling back reported the strength of the enemy. Battle formation followed with some sections moving on the flanks of the enemy. In a short time firing begun with blanks soon grew to a constant volume all along the line.

"The enemy was moving toward us, taking advantage of every shelter. They made an attempt to turn our left flank, but they were thwarted by Sergeant Pullman and Company D, (Grant Perkins was a member of that company). A half-hour double quick to our left, and the enemy soon faced heavy fire. They faltered and fell back. It was a running battle, and we were drawn well out of camp.

"The towering figure of Captain McGowan could be seen moving here and there, dexterously handling his chosen veterans. He was a wise old warrior, but he saw that escape was cut off for Gageby's men, hedging him in like a wedge. His men rallied around their commander and up went the white flag.

"Officers and men, mopping sweat from their faces, pressed forward to compliment the Captain and his boys for their gallant fight. It was an exciting day. We felt the Captain had failed in his boast, but there was a twinkle in his eye that did not belong to a man defeated.

"Suddenly, rapid firing was heard in the camp a long way

off. This lasted only a short time, and then all was still. McGowan turned to Gageby. 'Sir, you have me but I have your camp.'

"A small detachment of his men had approached the camp under cover of the river banks. Taking advantage of the battle on the other side, they had crept into the camp. Unobserved, they had fired on the camp guards who were on the wagons watching the progress of the battle.

"Major Gageby claimed that this force was not strong enough to do much damage and that, since the Captain and most of his men had been captured, Gageby's men had gained the victory. But the situation was ugly. The camp was in the possession of the enemy and the ammunition was spent. The camp and all of its supplies could be destroyed. The cost of re-taking it would be great. Captain McGowan's claim was true. He had taken the camp."

The article is posted, New York, 1905. Grant Perkins, the author, had by this time discarded the awkward name of Ulysses. The incident told in this story must have happened in September, 1893. Major Gageby's monthly report to the Army for that month says: "Companys B and D of the 12th Infantry under command of Major J.H. Gageby left the Fort in compliance with orders to field exercises on the borders of the Reservation September 21, 1893. The exercises consisted of short marches, instructions in the formation of camp, pitching, striking. and ditching of tents, loading and unloading wagons, cooking in the field, camp police, outpost duties, battalion drill, advance and rear guard action, and signalling with heliographs and flags. Miles marched 40." Discreetly, Major Gageby did not mention his "defeat".[25]

Chapter Ten

Fort "Swift Water"

It was the month of the "drying grass moon", October 22, 1894, when the 12th Infantry, dirty and tired from a twenty four hour train ride in packed coaches, stiffly formed up for the four mile march to Fort Niobrara at Valentine, Nebraska. Many looked longingly at the three saloons along the main street that straggled out into the prairie.

What they saw when they came across the wooden bridge over the Niobrara River, the river of swift water to the Sioux, was a replica of Fort Sully. The same adobe barracks, the huge parade ground, the canteen where liquor would soak up most of their pay, the officers quarters, and stables.

The Fort stood among the sandhills of northwestern Nebraska, and had been built about 1880 as an outpost near the Rosebud Reservation of the Sioux Indians to the north. The town was somewhat tamed in 1894. In an earlier year one of the officers "saw the body of a man hanging from a telegraph pole a short distance up the track". The station master had been angry, but not at the lynching. He said: "The people who hung that man last night had the nerve to put him in front of the station. By God, what would the passengers think of this town as they went by. The reputation of Valentine would be ruined. We cut him down and moved him up a pole or two."[26] The quintessence of the town booster.

In 1894 there were other small hardy shoots of institutions other than the saloons, five churches, several stores, and two newspapers. The *Valentine Republican* boasted in the October 12 issue that the Demo-Pops were on the run. It was referring to the Democrats who were populists, then strong in the west, fiercely agrarian and hostile to the east. It was wrong. The Democratic candidate for Congress from Nebraska won the November election in the wake of a severe depression.

The same issue reported that Gentleman Jim Corbett and the English fighter Fitzsimmons had agreed to a heavyweight championship fight at Jacksonville, Florida, for a purse of $10,000. Also that a shipment of $30,000 in silver, treaty payment to the Brule Sioux, had arrived by train and was escorted to the reservation by wagon, with guards. The Brule Sioux had been a proud and warlike tribe who could live in harmony with the plains as long as the buffalo were plentiful. From that shaggy beast they had their food, clothing, shelter, cooking fires from the dried dung, and parts of their religion.

But the buffalo were gone, and the Government now had treaty obligations to supply beef rations to the reservations. Government contractors drove cattle, some mere skin and bones, to the reservations, where, at several issue stations, the cattle were shot and the Indians cut and dried their portion of the meat. Their proud independence was at an end.

Grant was restless and tired of army life by now. He saw no prospect that things would be better at Fort Niobrara. The army was a dead-end street. With distaste he saw that Niobrara had a canteen and that there were many saloons at Valentine. That meant payday drunken brawls. His army experience made him an enemy of strong drink.

But there was someone at Fort Niobrara who made a big difference in Grant's life. Captain Orville Nave watched as the 12th Infantry marched in. As chaplain, he had charge of the post school, and wondered if there were any teachers among the men. Not likely, experience had taught him. He was a tall, soldierly-looking man with handle-bar moustache. He was a Methodist, an army career man.

Grant once wrote: "When I was 22, a member of the Ohio Conference (Methodist) reached out in an army barracks in Nebraska, and put the friendly arm of a minister around me. Within a year I was in school with a definite decision to become a minister."

Grant had come to Fort Niobrara without the excitement he had known first at Fort Sully. He was a veteran now —

at least a veteran of the boredom of garrison life. The officers had their careers, some social life, and sometimes even servants. The soldiers had the canteen, the town saloons, and the hope of getting out soon.

Martha Summerhayes, an army officer's wife, has told about life at Fort Niobrara.[27]

"The journey (from Arizona to Valentine) . . . was entirely by rail, across New Mexico and Kansas to St. Joseph, then up the Missouri River . . . finally we reached the small frontier town of Valentine. It was November and the drive across the rolling prairie gave us a glimpse of the country. The snow already lay on the brown and barren hills. The place struck a chill in my heart."

"We secured a colored cook who proved a very treasure. On inquiring how she came to be living in these wilds, I learned she had accompanied a young heiress who eloped with a cavalry lieutenant from her home in New York several years ago."

She described the winters. "With blood thinned down by the enervating summer at Tucson, here we were thrust into the polar regions. The mercury disappeared at the bottom of the thermometer. Enormous box stoves were in every room and the halls. Into these the soldiers stuffed great logs of mountain mahogany. The fires were kept roaring day and night."

But they ate well. "We could not complain about our fare, for our larder hung with all sorts of delicate and delicious things, brought in by the grangers (farmers) which we were glad to buy. Prairie chickens, young pigs, venison, and ducks, all hanging to be used when desired. To frappe a bottle of wine, we stood it on the porch. In a few minutes it would pour crystals."

And there were dances. "We had an excellent amusement hall with the chapel at one end and a good stage at the other. We had a good string orchestra of twenty pieces. As there were a number of active young bachelors (officers, of course) a series of dances were started. Never did I enjoy dancing more than at this time."

Grant and Captain Nave became close friends. Grant was often a guest in the Captain's home. He gave Grant a purpose in life when he most needed it. He also appointed Grant teacher in the Post school, although Grant was an unlikely candidate with only five years of school himself.

Maybe Grant would have found a way to get out of the army two years early without the help of Captain Nave, but I doubt it. In 1895 he still had two years to serve. One can only guess what strings were pulled, what letters were written, and what influence was brought to bear by Captain Nave that the last line of Grant's War Department record could be written: discharged October 21, 1895. Record excellent.

Again it was another October, a year after his arrival at Fort Niobrara. A little group stood waiting at the frontier station for the train that was to take Grant back to Kentucky again: Captain Nave, his diminutive wife, and their son, with whom Grant had become friends. He left his good friends bound for Barbourville, Kentucky, the site of Union College, "with a definite decision to become a minister". His life now had point and direction.

In the nineteen thirties, after the carnage of World War I, there was a strong peace movement in the Methodist Church. Conferences were sometimes asked to vote on resolutions to withdraw chaplains from the army, as anti-war gestures. Grant always fiercely opposed these moves. One can understand why. He knew what one chaplain had meant once to a lonely young soldier in a dreary frontier fort. He was remembering and honoring an old friend.

5. Drill at Fort Niobrara, Nebraska, about 1890
(From the John A. Anderson Collection at the
Nebraska State Historical Society, Lincoln, Nebraska
Used with permission)

6. Sioux Indians dancing on the Parade Grounds
Fort Niobrara, July 4, 1889
(From the John A. Anderson Collection at the
Nebraska State Historical Society, Lincoln, Nebraska)

7. Fort Niobrara, Valentine, Nebraska, about 1890
(From the John A. Anderson Collection at the
Nebraska State Historical Society, Lincoln, Nebraska)

Chapter Eleven

Mountain College

As the train to Barbourville, Kentucky, creaked and bounced back and forth, Grant joyfully took in the sights of the hills of his homeland. The oak and maple leaves were a rich brown and red on the mountain sides. After the barren prairies, he was glad to see the mountains and valleys again.

The train came to a noisy halt about a mile from the center of town. A horse streetcar was ready for its passengers. The old horse had his head down waiting patiently. The passengers climbed in, salesmen with their cloth bags, mountain men, a couple of new students to Union College. The passengers had to get off and give the old horse an extra shove on the steepest hill.

At the town square, the street circled around the courthouse, a graceless building stained with tobacco juice and hard use. The square was filled with wagons, horses, and people gathered for court, gossip, or trade.

Grant looked expectantly for the rising tower of Union College's one building. He went with a military bearing, the easy habit of three years in the army. He was excited and elated, joyfully anticipating his new life. When they are twenty-two and in any age the young feel the same elation. "I'm sitting on top of the world." " Life is just a bowl of cherries." "It's neat."

Reaching the campus, Grant made his way through about one hundred students, mostly mountain boys and girls. Union then enrolled only about ten in college courses. The rest were high school and even primary students, some in rough homespun mountain clothes, bewildered and homesick.

Grant had long ago gotten over that strange illness. He was now a well-traveled and experienced young man, and could talk knowingly about great cities, the west, and the Indians. But at twenty-two he had to start his formal education virtually from scratch, since as a boy he had very little schooling. In spite of later academic accomplishments, he was always sensitive about this. He once wrote me: "My education came late in life, hence a backwardness that came with my consciousness of a lack of education even after I was older than you are now." This feeling was partly the fuel for his drive to see that his children had the best in education.

He saw his cousin James B. Faulkner, a recent graduate and now a teacher and assistant to President of the college Daniel Stevenson. Grant's mother Elizabeth and Faulkner'a mother Samantha had been sisters. He found a room in town, since Union did not yet have a student dormitory, for which the weekly charge for room and board was $3.00. He paid a year's tuition of $45.00 out of his army savings of $8.00 a month.

In the six years between the autumn of 1895 and his graduation in June, 1901, he made friends in town and at the courthouse, did some writing for the *Mountain Advocate,* a Methodist religious paper, dropped out of school to earn money to continue, and immersed himself in learning. These were natural waters for him. One friend of those days was a young Barbourville lawyer, J.M. Robsion, later elected United States Senator from Kentucky.

How had Union College, this tiny beacon of light for the mountain young people, gotten started? For hundreds like it in America, the story of Union College was the story of one man of determination taking a big chance. As the frontier cut its way west, these little academias were far more important to America than the renowned Harvards and Yales.

Union had started in 1880 as a grade and high school, an alternative to the poorly supported public schools. Although backed by town leaders, the venture had failed, and in 1886 its property was to be sold at Sheriff's sale to pay the mortgage. Sadly, the experiment in education was over. But not quite. Sam Kelly, the converted soldier, the Methodist minister at Barbourville, talked to the delegates of the Annual Conference of the Methodist Episcopal Church North about buying Union for the church.

Dr. Daniel Stevenson, a well-known minister and then head of the Augusta Institute, another Methodist school, was a delegate to the Conference.[28] The Conference, with the timidity typical of such bodies, told Dr. Stevenson to "attend the sale without any authority to assume any financial obligation on behalf of the Conference". Armed with this timid mandate, Dr.Stevenson boldly decided to buy the college on his own and to present it to the next Annual Conference as an accomplished fact.

But how to do it? He had no money. Here we must bring on stage two quite different women, living hundreds of miles apart, Mahala Dowis and Fanny Speed. The richest person in Barbourville then was probably Mahala Dowis, whose husband had accumulated a considerable fortune during the Civil War. Green Elliott, the local druggist, "looked after" the affairs of widow Dowis, often escorting her to business and social affairs.

Dr. Stevenson arranged for Green Elliott to buy Union's property at the Sheriff's sale, with money to be furnished by Mrs. Dowis. It was to be a blind bid, one which does not reveal the name of the eventual buyer. Green Elliott bid in the property for $4425. Under Kentucky law, then, the sale could not become final for a year, giving a defaulting owner a year to pay up and redeem the property. So Dr. Stevenson knew he had a year in which to work on the men of the Annual Conference of the Methodists.

The men of the Conference never had a chance against that determined Scotsman. Stevenson at once drew up a paper "wherein it was agreed that the school should be reopened under my direction and under the patronage of the Kentucky Conference." Three weeks before the redemption date, the Conference took the plunge, authorizing Dr. Stevenson to raise the money if he should become the owner. It was as slick a deal as any corporate take-over in modern America, consummated as most of them are — entirely on borrowed money.

Now to introduce Fanny Speed, the other important woman in this story. She and Dr. Stevenson had been friends and church colleagues when he had earlier been minister at Trinity Methodist Church in Louisville, Kentucky. They had been a part of a failed attempt to re-unite the Southern and Northern Methodists Churches after the Civil War.

Stevenson had interested her in the college venture. Almost at once she gave $1000 and, within a few years, another $60,000. When she died in 1902 she left about $250,000, or half her estate, to the College, the bequest surviving a court test brought by the Henning heirs, as she had no children.

Who was she? As Fanny Henning, born in 1820, the daughter of a well-to-do family near Louisville, Kentucky, she married at twenty-five Joshua Speed who had just returned from Springfield, Illinois.

At the time of her wedding, she probably never knew that Joshua and a friend from Springfield, Illinois, had told "each other their secrets about women."[29] As Carl Sandburg tells it in *Abraham Lincoln, The Prairie Years,* "the wedding day of Speed and Fanny Henning had been set, and he was afraid he didn't love her; it was wearing him down; the date of the wedding loomed ahead of him as the hour of a sickly affair; he wrote Lincoln he was sick."[30]

Lincoln cheered him up with a long letter in which he referred to his own doubts about his marriage to Mary Todd. When the shoe had been on the other foot, Joshua had given advice to Lincoln.

If he did not love Mary, he should tell her so. Lincoln went to do just that. Again, Sandburg: "It was past eleven o'clock that night when he came back and said to Speed, 'When I told Mary that I did not love her, she burst into tears . . . It was too much for me. I found tears trickling down my cheeks. I caught her in my arms and kissed her."[31]

The deep friendship of Abraham Lincoln and Joshua and Fanny Speed lasted a lifetime. It had begun when the lanky new lawyer started his practice in 1837 in Springfield. He had bought a bed and bed clothes at Speed's store, on credit for $17. He had frankly told Speed that, if his experiment as a lawyer failed, he would probably not be able to pay. Joshua had afterwards said: "The tone of his voice was so melancholy that I felt for him . . . I never saw so gloomy and melancholy a face in my life."[32]

Their friendship deepened when he went with Joshua back to Kentucky after Speed had sold his store in Springfield. Lincoln mentioned this trip in his cheering letter. "Say candidly were not those heavenly black eyes the whole base of your early reasoning on the subject? Did you not go and take me all the way to Lexington and back for no other purpose than to get to see her again."[33]

After Joshua and Fanny had married, they decided to stay in Kentucky. Lincoln wrote sadly: "I regret to learn that you have resolved not to return to Illinois. I shall be very lonesome without you. How miserable things seem to be arranged in this world. If we have no friends, we have no pleasure and if we have them, we are sure to lose them and then be doubly pained by the loss. I did hope she and you would make your home here . . . "[34]

Fanny Speed had black eyes and glossy black hair. Her patrician face now looks out gently and thoughtfully at the students at Union who now pass but mostly ignore her portrait, busy with their own and the Twentieth century's problems.

Patrons of colleges like Fanny Speed tend to become unreal figures like statuary. Still, there was a human side to this story. Two uncertain young men (one to become the President and the other a wealthy businessman) made up an excuse for a long trip from Springfield, Illinois, to Lexington, Kentucky, so that one of them could see the beautiful black-eyed Fanny Henning again and have the moral support of his friend.

If he had known this story, Grant would have been glad that Joshua and Fanny Speed decided not to return to Springfield, even if they had to disappoint Abraham Lincoln. When Dr. Stevenson was signing a note to buy a college, and Fanny Speed was backing the venture, Grant Perkins, fourteen, was hoeing corn and doing farm chores and reading the *Youth's Companion.* He was beginning to dream dreams. He was unaware that a college would be ready for him years later in that sea of illiteracy in the mountains. Its course offerings, compared to the rich variety in an American university now, would be meagre. But what a difference in his life that spare diet will make.

Looking back at the whole story, one feels that the fragile threads of these lives were knit together to make one whole strong cloth. Mrs. Dowis with her silks and fans, Green Elliott at her side; Dr. Stevenson the indomitable; Fanny Speed, the generous widow of Abraham Lincoln's best friend; and the boy Grant, with a mind wide-awake, coming out of the mountains; somehow all are one, all alive, all immortal. Nothing has really died. Maybe that is immortality enough.

8. Fanny Henning Speed
Benefactor of
Union College
Wife of Joshua Speed,
Abraham Lincoln's
best friend
(From a portrait at
Union College
which was painted
from a photograph
about 1855)

9. James P. Faulkner
Grant's cousin and
President of
Union College in 1901

Chapter Twelve

Cavalry Captain

The quiet rhythm of his little mountain academia totally absorbed Grant until the spring of 1898. For many years the crisis over Cuba, then in Spanish hands, had been hovering over the country, like heat lightning on the horizon of a tranquil night.

Cuba had been enough of an issue to be included in the platforms of both major political parties in 1896. While the Democrats extended their sympathy to the Cubans, the Republicans promised "to restore peace and to give independence to the island."[35] Just how that was to be done without war was never explained.

The heat lightning burst into thunder on February 15, 1898, when the battleship Maine sank in explosions and flames in Havana harbor. Whether the initial small explosion was internal (coal dust) or external has never been determined. But no doubt the initial explosion set off the forward powder magazine, and the second explosion sank the Maine.

Under the slogan "Remember the Maine", the country erupted into demands for war. Nudged along by the Hearst newspapers, America was rushing cheerfully into war.

But President William McKinley was no war hawk. He persuaded a new and more liberal Spanish government to meet most of the demands of the United States. He tried hard to quiet the war fever. He knew that the army, scattered in small units around the country like Grant's 12th Infantry, was not at all prepared for war. By contrast, the Navy, spurred by a young and energetic assistant Secretary, Teddy Roosevelt, was well prepared, as its victories proved.

For a short time peace had a chance. William Randolph Hearst's *New York Journal* had sent the famous painter of western scenes, Frederic Remington, to Cuba. Remington wanted to come home, reporting there would be no war. Hearst wired back: "Please remain. You furnish the pictures. I will furnish the war."[36]

But President McKinley felt no euphoria about the prospect of war. Even though he worked hard at a diplomatic solution, he was beleaguered by his own party in Congress. There is a poignant scene in Margaret Leech's book *In The Days of McKinley* which shows his torment. Leech writes: "McKinley had been unable to sleep. In desperate need for rest he had vainly taken narcotics. His face had grown seamed and haggard and sunken, with dark circled eyes ... To a few visitors he talked of his dread of suffering that war entailed. At the end of March, while a musicale was taking place in the East Room, he withdrew for a short time into the Red Parlor with Mr. Kohlstaat. (editor of the *Chicago Times Press* and an early McKinley supporter) He sat ... on the large crimson brocade lounge, rested his head on his hands, and poured out his distress, protesting that Congress was trying to drive the country into war, that the armed services were not prepared; talking too of his sleepless nights and his worries about Mrs. McKinley's health. He burst into tears as he spoke."[37]

But in spite of his mostly successful diplomatic efforts, Congress pushed the issue on McKinley. On April 20, 1898, in a brazen usurpation of a President's constitutional duty to conduct foreign affairs, the Congress declared the independence of Cuba by joint resolution. Spain had no other choice of honor but to break relations. Congress declared war on April 25. As a quick fix to expand the army swiftly, Congress also passed an Act on April 22, authorizing governors of the states to appoint officers who would then raise volunteer companies.

The war fever spread quickly to Barbourville and to Union College, as can be seen from the following swift sequence of events recorded in the small clear hand of a War Department copyist.[38] "Troop A lst Volunteer calvary from Kentucky was organized by Captain U.S.G. Perkins at Barbourville, Ky.

May 3, 1898... Was mobilized at Lexington, May 11, 1898. The troop consists of the finest horsemen that were living in the region from which they came."

Think of the speed of it, the directness of the action, the absence of red tape, the Minute Men born again. Within three weeks of the passage of the enabling act, Grant Perkins had his appointment as captain from Governor William O. Bradley; and had recruited and transported to Lexington, 123 miles away, an entire eager company of volunteers. I am certain that in a few days he had emptied Union College of most of its young men.

For him the pleasures of Latin, geology, philosophy, and literature were temporarily replaced by the pleasures of command. But war did not mean to him what it means to us today. He had not seen whole cities pulverized in two World Wars, or millions cremated because of their race. He never knew about the docile atom, stung into its deadly rage by the genius of man. He only felt the excitement and false romance of command and war. For a poor mountain boy, the prestige was heady stuff. He once told me he was one of the youngest officers in that war.

Company A soon arrived at Fort Thomas in Georgia, the huge headquarters of the First Army Corps, Department of the Gulf. Company B had also arrived from Saylorsville, Kentucky, and Grant was appointed to command that company also. Now the extent of the War Department's unpreparedness for war became glaringly clear, just as President McKinley had feared. It was easy to get volunteers but not so easy to equip them. Grant's company was still at Fort Thomas in July, and "the troop had only been equipped partly in clothing and horses, the ordnance stores not yet having arrived."[39] The rapid increase of the army had simply swamped the War Department.

Perhaps at a meeting of cavalry officers, somehow during this period, he met Teddy Roosevelt, commander of the Rough Riders, an outfit specially authorized by Congress to recruit the western cowboys outside the regular army. Colonel Leonard Wood, the White House Physician, and Roosevelt, assisant secretary of the Navy, had the political clout to get this command. They were also aggressive and abrasive in getting their supplies; and many a regular army field commander, left to flounder helplessly in The War Department's confusion, must have roundly cursed these two free-wheeling mavericks.

Grant and his boys had marched from Barbourville in May in glorious anticipation of freeing Cuba, fighting for their country, and having fun doing it. In August they were still stuck in Fort Thomas without their guns, and the war was for all practical purposes over. Bottled up in Havana Harbor, the Spanish fleet was destroyed on July 3rd. Spain was unable afterward to relieve its forces or to get them new supplies. As the volunteers poured into Fort Thomas, sanitary conditions collapsed. Typhoid fever and malaria were epidemic. Called camp fever during the Civil War, typhoid by this time was preventable; its causes were polluted water and food. The Army Surgeon General, George Sternberg, had given orders as to its control, but never checked to see if his orders were being carried out.

There were about 40,000 men at Fort Thomas. By August, 10,000 had come down sick and about 700 had died. Secretary of War Alger sent an aide to investigate. He was so dismayed at what he found that he ordered the army to abandon the camp.[40] Its soldiers were no longer needed, anyhow.

If boredom and frustration did not get Grant and his boys, typhoid and malaria probably would. In Grant's case, it was malaria, a disease which troubled him periodically for many years thereafter. The monthly attendance record of the War Department tells the final chapter of Company A. "Troop A and B, First Kentucky Cavalry left Fort Thomas, Kentucky, pursuant to special orders, August 29, for Camp Hamilton, Lexington, Ky."[41] Shaken by malaria, Grant arrived back in Kentucky. For him the war was over before it started.

Spain had asked for terms in August, and the war formally ended in October. Its end brought angry charges of bad food, disease, and incompetence.

The wild confusion of much of this war can be seen in what happened to the Rough Riders. On the train to Tampa, food ran out and the officers had to buy food with their own money. At Tampa, they had to abandon their horses, because there was no transport for them and because the Cuban terrain made it impossible for them to function as cavalry, anyhow. Nobody in the army had figured that out before. Finally, to get to Cuba at all, they had to commandeer a ship that had been assigned to another army unit. They did this by double quick marching on board before the other unit could get there and then refusing to budge. Even at that only 500 of its troop ever got to Cuba to storm San Juan Hill in what has probably been the most over ballyhooed battle in American military history.[42]

But the wonder of it is that any troops at all got to Cuba in the short time since war had been declared. It was a gayly scrambled and improvised war which we won more because of the weakness of Spain than because of the strength of America. It cost us in a few months 250 million dollars, and brought us an empire in the Pacific which we hardly knew what to do with. The human cost was about 400 men lost in battle and 5000 lost to disease.

The world then tolerated some human inefficiency, even in war. The bureaucrat, the computer, the flow chart, the logical structure of the multi-national corporation or of the Marxist state, had not yet compressed us into their authoritative, efficient, and unforgiving molds.

Grant Perkins, organizing his own company of volunteers, and Teddy Roosevelt, commandeering his own ship at Tampa, were individual free-wheeling acts of a similar nature. Grant may have sensed this when he wrote once during World War I about the differences between Germany and America. "America flourishes on freedom and inefficiency." In the Archives, the final report about Captain Grant Perkins shows that he was discharged October 14, 1898, was paid off, but owed the United States $5.17 for arms and equipment, probably for the sword that hung for so many years on the wall of his study at home. I wonder if he ever paid them. Even though his only enemy had been malaria and frustration, he arrived again on the campus at Union, a hero of sorts.

10. Captain U. S. G. Perkins
Troop A First Kentucky Volunteer Cavalry
Spanish-American War, 1898

Chapter Thirteen
The Valedictory

June, 1901. The Commencement Exercises at Union College. Grant stood first in his class, but then the graduates were only Grant Perkins and Will Harris. You knew that an army man had coined the class motto: "Forward march follows mark time". Grant's cousin, J. B. Faulkner, now the president since the death of Dr. Stevenson, handed out the diplomas. Grant was 28.

A few pages in his own handwriting give an insight into the maturation of his mind in the five years since he first came to Barbourville. The mind deserves its biography also.

On first coming to Union, Grant had copied a humorous poem. It was "The Classical Preacher" about a Welshman who passed off the cadences of his native language as classical Greek onto his unsuspecting congregation until one day he spotted another Welshman in the pews.

"Then Welshman in pulpit to Welshman in pew,
In the barbarous dialect they alone knew,
Cried: 'Friend, by the land of our fathers, I pray
As you hope for salvation, don't give me away.'
The joke was so rich, the old Welshman kept still
And the classical parson is preaching there still."

His handwriting is labored, juvenile, and uncertain, as though he is just learning to write again after years in the army.

Five years later, his valedictory, *The Ethical End of Man*, is clearly and legibly written in simple and grammatical sentences.

He had certainly seen enough drunkenness, sin and sorrow in the mountains and the army to know that the ethical was not the natural world of man. Yet he believed in that eventual role for mankind without doubt or cynicism. Perhaps he saw our role as it could be, and not photographically with all the warts.

He begins: "The geologist in his search through nature's treasures finds man the highest result of a creative power which is not his province to explain . . . capable of every development and high attainment, whether physical, moral, social, intellectual, or spiritual."

Clearly, he had studied geology and was well acquainted with the idea that man had slowly emerged out of a dim past. "Man is the culmination of a creation that extends far back into the misty past, the work of infinite ages."

The earlier ages had produced nothing lasting, but something extraordinary had happened to the species called man. "Man passed through the ordeal . . . with a creative responsibility that made him not only the keeper of the outer world but the master of the inward one which broadens into eternity. To him was given to invest nature in her choicest shroud and his heart toward spiritual immortality."

He was comfortable with the idea that the evolutionary growth of man was in harmony with God's purposes. Today, the whole issue of evolution is boiling up again in the courts, this time as creationist science, after a lull of fifty years. Grant in 1901 believed: why, indeed, cannot God create in a slow and maturing way as well as by fiat and a rib transplant. I am certain that, in that moment, he believed both in the Bible and Science, and the simplistic excommunication of one by the other was not a part of his glowing synthesis.

One can feel his intellectual excitement as he worked on his address. The oil lamp gave off an unsteady light and the soft sounds of a June night came through the open window of his room as he eagerly chased his own glowing thoughts. When you are young, such moments of spiritual and intellectual discovery are the finest in life. Of course, his was not a new discovery at all, but it was his purest pleasure to have thought so.

A society like ours today really cheats us when it tells us

in a thousand ways that pleasure is only libidinous and sensual. Grant did not have the disadvantage of living in the television age under such a continuous bombardment. He knew that pleasure was also intellectual and spiritual.

In his address he was impressed with inventive genius of man. In those days all were astonished at the inventions that were crowding in on us. Even so, two that would change the face of the earth had hardly happened at all in 1901. The internal combustion engine, first developed by two Frenchmen, Charles and Frank Duryea, was still only a plaything. And we were still two years away from the Wright brothers' flight at Kitty Hawk in 1903.

If you add to the multiplying inventions the idea that progress for man was going to be easy, natural, and painless, you have the base in our trust now in progressive technology as the savior of the world. The idea of technology as God may now be crashing into unperceived or misunderstood limitations.

But in his paper Grant did not see technology as the true goal of man. "Apart from the outer world with all its possibilities for improvement, there is the inward world, one more lasting. The ethical world lies before every individual. The soul can enjoy it as it develops from the material toward the spiritual. It is a land of pure delight."

Men are like the young eagle. "The eaglet, seeing its mother in the distant space above, knows that the narrow nest is not its home and, with a wild scream of joy, it spreads its untried pinions and soars away in those aerial regions ordained for its home."

As I closed the notebook where I kept the brittle pages written over eighty years ago, I was glad for at least a glimpse into his young mind and passion. He could not have forseen that man's admired technology has not "invested nature in her choicest shroud". But just as America in 1901 was young and confident of its destiny, he was a young man just discovering God and his own mind and intellect. In any age these are cherished moments.

Chapter Fourteen
Diary Of A Voyage

It is May 3rd, 1905. Spring has come to New York City. Battery Park, looking out to sea, is full of soft sunlight and greening trees. For a year Grant has been in dirty and exciting New York City as associate minister of Grace Methodist Church in Manhattan.

After his graduation from Union in 1901, he had worked as managing editor of *The Mountain Advocate,* a small religious magazine in Middleboro, Kentucky. It was an impressive title until one learns that his chief job was to sell job printing. He had left Middleboro in September, 1902, for the Methodist Conference at Louisville, Kentucky, where "he did not have a pleasant time and was left without appointment (to a church) to attend school."

School meant Drew Theological Seminary (now Drew University) in Madison, New Jersey, which in 1866 had been given to the Methodists, complete and paid for by Daniel Drew, one of the robber baron Wall Street figures of the times.[43] Enthusiastically, Grant kept adding courses, "If I keep this up, I will pass this course in two instead of three years." He did.

Drew Seminary was then so well endowed that costs were very low. There was no charge at all for tuition, room rent, or library. In the dormitory the only charge was $35 a year for heat, electric, care of room, and incidentals. $3.00 a week fed Grant.[44] At Drew he became a top student, his mind well-honed. At the completion of the course for a degree of Bachelor of Divinity in 1904, he won one of the top honors — The European Fellowship.

He wrote of those days. "Toward the close of my last year at Drew, I became the assistant pastor of Grace Church. Postponing my fellowship for a year, I submitted to the liberalizing hammers of Columbia University."

He had known the simple and primitive religion of the mountains, the stern classicism of Dr. Stevenson at Union College (who had once given the Commencement address in Latin), and the endless exegesis of the Old and New Testaments at Drew, where the course offerings simply ignored the blazing social, ethical, and industrial problems of the day.

In Columbia and New York City, his quiet stream in life entered the rapids of intellectual and social change. Nicholas Murray Butler, as president of Columbia, was expanding the graduate departments and was luring famous educators and philosophers to New York. In all of America in 1900 there were only 6000 graduate students in all fields.

Reform and change were in the very air, and old ways were being vigorously challenged. Teddy Roosevelt, as unlikely a Republican as ever lived in the White House, had won a big victory in the Supreme Court in 1904, which broke up the railroad "trusts" in the Northern Securities case.

But even though he was a maverick reformer himself, he was still highly critical of journalistic reformers like Lincoln Steffens and Ida Tarbell, calling them muckrakers after the man in *Pilgrim's Progress,* who was so busy raking muck off the floor that he could not even look up but only down.[45] These were disturbing, fluid, and exciting times. Grant could hardly escape these swift currents.

I can only guess what else Grant did in America's most sophisticated city in that year. Because his delight in learning had never abated, I am not surprised that he studied at Columbia. I am sure he saw some baseball games of the New York Giants, who had recently completed their stadium at the Polo Grounds and were playing to 40,000 fans a game.

He always liked baseball. Later when we lived at Massillon, Ohio, in the 1920's, we regularly went to the home games of the Massillon Agathons, a minor league semi-professional team. Still later in Cleveland, he had a ministerial pass to the Cleveland Indians games at old League Park. Sometimes I used it myself. The gatekeeper must have been skeptical of so adolescent a man of the cloth.

I am sure he may have gone to see some of the plays in New York, because he never warned me about the evils of the theatre, but seemed relaxed about those supposed devils. Americans were eager for entertainment in 1904, and New York City was the hub of it all. A new play opened on Broadway almost every day. The vaudeville houses were usually full. The Floradora girls were very popular. Comedians Fields and Weber had them laughing in the aisles. Maude Adams was a piquant Peter Pan.

A new form of entertainment came to New York in 1903 — the movies. *The Great Train Robbery* was filmed in the freight yards of the Lackawanna Railroad in Patterson, New Jersey, in that year.

The plays were mostly still suitable for a young Methodist minister, but a few were too strong for a late Victorian morality. In one play, *The City,* the words God Damn were used for the first time on stage. "The audience rose in such a horror and hysteria that the *New York Sun* critic fainted dead away in the crush."[46] But I am sure of one thing. He never entered the famous ornate bars of New York, for he hated alcohol. In this he was Methodist to the core.

But his year in New York was over, and he was now looking forward to his great adventure, traveling in Europe and studying in Leipzig University in Imperial Germany.

So it was that on this day in May, 1905, a party of happy young people had come to the pier to say bon voyage to their minister at Grace Church. Grant was no longer a raw mountain boy. At the age of 32, with a full beard, he was an educated man with a definite charm.

This spring day ships solidly lined the piers along the Hudson and East Rivers. It was the zenith of the steamship. The tall black bow of his ship loomed above Grant. The pier was a confused jumble of crates, cargo, sweating longshoremen, passengers, friends, and their luggage. The ship was The Statendam, ten thousand tons of Dutch seaworthiness, her destination Boulogne-Sur-Mer in France and Rotterdam in Holland. Grant's second class passage cost $52.50.[47]

Among his friends on the pier that day was a girl who had brought a going-away present. Among the odds and ends of papers I found after his death was a note that had once been attached to a package. A clear female hand had written:

*"When far removed from sight of land
With hours of idleness on hand
In place of spoons your fingers take
And eat this up for old time's sake."*

Since I know he was never again to be "far removed from sight of land", I am certain this little verse dates from that day in May, 1905. Perhaps he kept this trifle because he still remembered the girl who brought her present to him.

As The Statendam moved slowly down the river and into the harbor and sea, he watched the city and the Statue of Liberty sink slowly into the horizon and turned his attention to the little shipboard world.

On the first day out, he fell into a conversation with a Russian consular officer of the Czar. Even though he disliked him almost at once, he listened to him because he wanted to know more about that strange and almost mythical land. In January, 1905, he had read about the bloody Sunday killing of over five hundred peaceful demonstrators by the Cossacks in Petrograd (now Leningrad). This had drawn a storm of protest from the west and had provoked the usually gentle Mark Twain in his *Czar's Soliloquy* to call for the overthrow of the Czar.

On the first day Grant wrote: "He (the consul) has an unpleasant habit of laughing in a silly way after finishing a sentence. But I hope to find out something of the internal condition of Russia through this man. He told me that the Slav and the Jew could not live together. The Jew was too smart for the Slav and hence would never get any freedom in Russia." How little has changed since 1905 in this respect.

The next morning Grant had recovered from the rush and excitement of his preparations for going, and, he exulted at the wonderful thing that was happening to him. He wrote, "Good morning, good ship, people, mighty waters, sky, sunshine, and love. How beautiful. How majestic! Here we are 300 miles from New York and alone with God and the sea. My soul is full, my heart light, my joy supreme, my expectations bright. I slept like a child, was up early, had a good breakfast with a good appetite, and now for the day. The weather is fine and clear, the sky blue with scarcely any wind. The ship is a good sailor, broad and steady."

I leave him standing in the bright May morning at sea. Any words of mine would be wooden to describe such a song of joy.

The sea held the rapt attention of this young man from the mountains. "I'm quite at home with the sea and the sky. The world of ocean waves could be my delight forever."

Observing his fellow passengers in second class, he wrote: "They are, for the most part, Germans, Swiss, and Hollanders who came over a few years ago in steerage and are now going back to visit their relatives." In the saloon the orchestra played and the beer flowed freely, he disapprovingly noted. As were many Americans then, he was not very kind to immigrants from the Old World. He wrote of those he saw, "God may have made all men equal, but there has been some slipping somewhere".

On Sunday the steward had discovered there was a minister on board and asked Grant to preach. Apprehensively, he consented. "These people have been taught differently about religion than I." But he need not have worried. "The services passed off pleasantly, all coming in."

He also met a friend that day, ". . . a very interesting young man, Minor Sarto, an artist from New York. He is working his way and is a fine fellow. His experiences have been much like my own, and he is of the same daring temperament."

In the next few days, he settled into the tranquil routine of any sea voyage in good weather, watching the waters and the people, even hoping for a storm. "I suppose I shall not be storm wiser after this voyage. Yet a storm must be majestic here in the middle of the Atlantic."

He reflected on "how varied are the ways of men. Yet we, in our different ways, as on a ship, are closely bound together." He felt sorry for a flock of birds which had apparently been driven seaward by a storm somewhere and were beyond their capacities to reach land again.

On the eighth day Grant saw sea gulls from land, as they passed Scilly Island, and were into the English Channel full of shipping. Ten days after leaving New York, he reached the Hook of Holland and took a train to Rotterdam. Here his enthusiasm bubbled over again. "On land and in a Dutch Hotel, and going to sleep in a Dutch bed. I saw something of the city this afternoon and evening and am now ready for sleep. But this Dutch bed: It looks like a Dutchman (probably a featherbed). And when the door is closed, you cannot tell where it is. They have not discovered gas or electricity yet. My, how slow these people are! One would think they have all eternity at their disposal. But that is their way and I should not complain."

I can see the American character in that passage. Impatience. Impatient to clear new land as his great grandfather Solomon had done in Kentucky in 1817. Impatient to go west as his brother George had done in 1889. Impatient to complete a three year course in two as he had done at Drew. Impatient with the Dutch because they had not yet installed electric lights in his hotel room.

I could have reminded him that, from 1817 until the days of his own youth, his people had cooked their food over an open fireplace and never even owned a stove. Someone could have correctly said about them, "My, how slow these people are."

11. Grant as a student in Germany, 1905

12. The Dutch steamship, Statendam, on which Grant sailed to Rotterdam and Europe, May 5, 1905 (Photo courtesy The Mariner's Museum, Newport News, Virginia)

Chapter Fifteen

Traveler In Europe

After his first night in a Dutch bed, Grant "had to wake the sleepy landlord to get out of his house. Came to the Hague early, got breakfast, did the town, and left for Leyden where I repeated the same thing. The cities are all in a file, and a good walker can soon get over them."

But this was a strange and almost unnatural land to him. "The country is level and low, and cut by numerous canals. One does not see cattle on a thousand hills but in low fields with water all around and above them. This funny, flat, little land." He had known the tall forests of the mountains and the continental plains. He was comfortable there and not in the tiny miniature of Holland.

He arrived in Amsterdam on Sunday. "I found tonight that the public drinking houses are filled with men and women and blue with smoke. The streets are crowded and boisterous. After I went to my room, I could not sleep for companies of drunken fellows making all kinds of noise. If this is a continental Sunday, I want none of it." In his boyhood, as rip-roaring as the mountains could be, Sunday at least was strictly Sabbath, and mostly spent in the unpainted Bear Creek Chapel. He had no appreciation of a European Sunday as a day of pleasure.

At Cologne on May 15, he wrote about the famous cathedral there. It "is one of Germany's relics. Of course, it is not useful and never was as to that. But it is a real curio." Before I accuse him of being insensitive before one of the most famous of all cathedrals, I remember my own first sight of it in August, 1969. Immense smoke blackened spires, more overpowering than beautiful. A monument to the intense medieval preoccupation with God, but hardly a pleasant place in which to worship, such as Old North Church in Boston, with its sunny pews and white columns, still is.

There he attended his first church service in Europe. A Catholic service, its Latin symbolism was incomprehensible. The priests and the people were tiny insignificant figures under the stone arches far above them. In the Middle Ages this had invoked the feeling of an awesome God, but God to Grant was closer and more familiar. He was too close to the provincial isolation of the mountains fully to appreciate that Latin had been a unifying force of the medieval international church.

From Cologne to Bonn, where he took a Rhine River steamer to Binghen, he was a typical American tourist, determined to miss nothing. On May 16, "I reached this place (Binghen) after a day full of interest on the Rhine. The constant panorama of natural scenery, history, romance, and legend spread before me all day has quite intoxicated me. The swelling in my heart cannot be written down on paper." But then a typically American remark, "But after all, the Rhine falls far short of the Hudson."

At last on May 18, he arrived at Leipzig, the capitol of Saxony, fifteen days, an ocean, and eleven cities after leaving New York. "Fully tired out. A rest will now do me good. I have a room and now for some rest and then university and study." But on Sunday he looked for and found a Methodist chapel in that strange far-away city. He wrote about it in a lovely fragment of a sermon which I found among his papers. It is called *Spiritual Unity.*

"The last church service I attended was in New York City almost a month ago. Since then, an ocean had been crossed, and I had become a traveling fiend and had buried myself in the continent of Europe. Strange faces and unknown tongues had been my constant companions. I had bartered with shopkeepers, quarreled with bus drivers and with guides and hotel clerks.

"But it was over, thank God, and a beautiful Sunday morning found me in the city of philosophy and classical learning. As I went my lonely way through the broad avenues and shady parks, the birds were engaged in their morning service of song and worship. I then remembered that I, too, am a Christian and must kindle devotional altars and send up spiritual incense.

"Turning from those who were worshipping in God's out-of-doors, I looked for a humbler altar at which to kneel. Turning down a side street and passing through a small alley and a court filled with the first flowers of spring, I went into a small 'Salle" or hall where the little German Methodist congregation worshipped. At the door I was given a warm handshake and a Methodist hymnal and was taken to a seat near the front. I was at home.

"All was so quiet. The people came in, took their seats and leaned forward in silent prayer. The minister knelt behind the pulpit. The hymns were heartily sung. The prayer lifted my hungry homesick soul to the Throne of Grace. The scriptures were read with earnest expression. The sermon was full of power but all in German. Jesu Christu and his holy character was the theme. No cumbersome manuscript or notes burdened the wings of thought. The minister was adept with the sword of the spirit.

"In forty minutes I forgot the heathen life I had led in the past month, forgot my lonesomeness, forgot irritability, and felt myself again a child of God. I am Christ's. My soul was full, and I thanked God that in a distant land, I could worship in a Methodist house with Methodist people. I could hardly understand a word of what was said, and only with difficulty talk to the good minister after the service. But what matter. The Spirit is one and interprets not the words of the tongue but the messages of the soul."

Even though Grant understood German imperfectly, the force of the scriptures and the sermon came through to him.

Chapter Sixteen

Leipzig University

Leipzig was then the cultural capitol of Saxony, a small monarchy which had first been pressed into the folds of Prussia and then Imperial Germany by Bismark. Its ancient university was respected throughout the world.

Grant had a letter of introduction to a woman who ran a boarding house or "pension." He took a room there. Grant wrote in his diary, "Her father had been mixed up in the Rhenish Rebellion (a part of the failed European revolution of 1848), had fled to America, fought later in the Civil War, and was a friend of Abraham Lincoln."

Far from being a lover of freedom herself, she became a Teutonic female tyrant who tried to take complete charge of his life. He felt she must have been hired by the police to watch every move of his. She was his first, but not last, encounter with the nineteenth-century German mind. They clashed even on minor matters. They had a running battle about polishing his shoes, a task she insisted should be done by women and not by gentlemen.

And so in June, after a side trip to Hamburg, Berlin, and Wittenberg, the latter Luther's birthplace, he wrote, "Today I made a change in my lodgings, I hope for the better. I had never realized before there could be such disagreeable persons, but my landlady took the cake. I couldn't sit down, get up, or turn around but she must know the reasons."

His first irritation with the German state came after he had registered at the University. In the mountains, unless you were moonshining, you might not see the county sheriff for years. But in Germany then the police knew where everyone

lived and worked. He wrote, "That same afternoon, Fraulein hustled me to the police station where I had to register again and was given a 'schein' which I must carry or be fined 50 marks. His imperial highness behind the desk knew all there was to know about me before he was through with me. In America one must be a crook to get into the Rogues' Gallery, but in Germany every resident and citizen belongs there as a matter of right. When I left for Rome, I even had to give him my place of residence in Rome and the train I was to leave on. The Prussian police hold their hand over every citizen. I have protested to many Germans, but they think it is right and proper. Germany is the most thoroughly policed state in the world."

His sense of personal freedom was offended even by the minor requirement that he register with the police. And why not? He was an alien, a stranger. Maybe in the isolated mountains a stranger was rarely seen, but in nineteenth century America as we moved west, strangers were the norm.

Americans have always been impatient of any hindrance. We accept the state highway police only surlily. But the feeling was in the bones of our geography. When you can breathe the fragrant spring on the Blue Ridge Parkway and the dry air of Arizona within a few days, there is an exhilaration which Europeans within their cramped boundaries cannot feel.

Grant's second disappointment was with the University. He wrote: "I had been led to believe that the best in education was in Germany. The man who could parenthesize his degree with the name of a German University held center stage." His excitement in going to Germany was intellectual. What castles in the air he had built in expectation.

He described the classroom. "All preliminaries were attended to by a go-between who acted as a servant to the professor. If a student had some personal matter or question, he must go to the mediary who would present it to his excellency the professor. You never talked to him personally. The way he stood beyond and above us rubbed my inbred Americanism."

He saw there was a difference between American and German scholarship. "I know the German system has its advantages. It is the concentration on a very small point that counts here. In America we are broad. In Germany deep. In Germany when a student has dug up the final word, he is anchored to his buoy for the rest of his days. The German doctorate is a needle point that has punctured the thick skin of ignorance in one tiny place. This makes the German professor narrow and may explain some peculiar positions he has taken of moral significance."

He described the library. "I had received a list of books to read for my classroom work. The librarian referred me to twenty large index volumes. I was to get the section and shelf number, leave the list with him, and call for them in three days. The clumsy volumes were in German script, often unintelligible. They were the only index of authors and their subjects. Shades of Dewey." (The Dewey Decimal system of library organization.)

Then dueling. This anachronism of a civilized nation completely turned him off. Even though long banned in America, he found that in Germany the Government encouraged it.

"This held an important place in the school and was encouraged by the school authorities and the government. The sword was drawn almost nightly. For the least trivial offense the challenge was sent, accepted, seconds chosen, and the fight was on until blood was drawn. When the spirit of dueling lagged, committees were appointed to select students to fight and to see that it was carried out. This is Germany's pet diversion and is supposed to stimulate the fighting blood.

"The custom is popular among the students, and a scar in an affair of honor is a special mark of valor, shown to his mother, sister, or sweetheart with great pride." But Grant sensed also that there was some hokum and comic opera about this juvenile custom for a nation. "The young man lets it be known that he has an affair of honor and makes a visit home or writes to say farewell. He makes a disposition of his personal effects. But few deaths are reported. While there is some danger, many of the young bloods 'threw off' a great deal during the fight. If wounded, he would seclude himself for a few days until his wounds began to heal, but he was careful to have all his bandages in plain sight."

He found Prussian militarism everywhere and especially in Berlin which he visited twice. "For days I tramped her streets, visited her museums and art galleries, mingled with the crowds in their beer gardens, enjoyed her theatres and music, and breathed her martial air. I heard their boasts about Deutschland Uber Alles."

He did not like the way women were treated in Germany. "The German father and husband is lord of all he surveys. To help in the home or to notice his own children is a sign of weakness. I once saw a German mother run into a store leaving her baby with her husband. The baby began to cry. The husband, fearing that someone would think it his baby, crossed the street until his wife came out. He then re-crossed the street, and I have never heard a poor woman get such a tongue lashing for leaving him exposed as the caretaker of his own child."

He wrote: "It was my privilege to travel all over the Empire. Everywhere in the fields the women out numbered the men ten to one. I saw them trimming the vines along the Rhine, planting potatoes along the Maine, or harvesting wheat along the Oder. They are also in the factories, and here is one of the reasons for the cheapness of articles made in Germany which has so disturbed the old channels of trade in world commerce." His reference was to the intense competition that Germany was giving England in the years before World War I.

The last entry in his German diary in September, 1905, summarizes his feelings. "I leave early tomorrow on my way down to Rome. I have learned to dislike everything German. The Emperor (Kaiser Wilhelm II of World War I) may talk all he pleases about Germany's mission to enlighten and civilize the world, but I don't think folks will take it seriously. They think they are in the swim, but Americans could teach them many things. Tomorrow I quit "der Vaterland", and I am glad of it."

When I told Dr Otto Plaut, a friend from Canton, Ohio, that Grant did not like Leipzig University and Germany in 1905, he was pained. As a small boy then, growing up in Leipzig, he remembered it as a place of beauty and serenity. But even though he had been a product of that culture, as a Jew he had been run out of his native land by Hitler's savage storm troopers. Perhaps Grant's insights as a student about

Germany were more accurate than Dr. Plaut's nostalgic memories.

Grant had expected so much and had found a strange dichotomy. He later wrote about those days: "One need not be astonished at peculiar things here. In this land of freedom and despotism, scholarship and ignorance, advance and stagnation, three centuries live side by side."[48]

Maybe his was an unfairly harsh and simplistic judgment. Americans rarely try to understand the countries they visit, but at least he had other reasons than bad plumbing for his opinions.

He may also have sensed the dark Teutonic tribe beneath the elegant exterior and the Prussian imprint on the land. No nation is ever far removed from its darker side and must always be wary of it. As Bruce Catton has observed, this is also true of America. "There is a rowdy strain in American life, living close to the surface but running very deep. Like an ape behind a mask, it can display itself suddenly with terrifying effect."[49]

Grant's uncomplicated feelings about Imperial Germany may help explain what happened to Germany under Hitler. There must be some hidden reason why a Germany that produced and nurtured Beethoven and Goethe could also in our times produce the horrors of the human furnaces.

Chapter Seventeen
The Bishop And The Student

Grant was surprised that, in 1905, a tiny but sturdy minority of Methodists was firmly in place all over Europe. Bishop William Burt had been put in charge of the European Parish in 1904, and, in that year alone, had traveled over 20,000 miles visiting churches in his parish. His report for 1905 listed 53,000 members and 492 preachers.[50]

Both the Bishop and the student believed, perhaps unrealistically, that their beloved church was the evangelical wave of the future. The Bishop: "We have publishing houses, hospitals, schools of all grades, and valuable property in each of these nations. We have already become a spiritual force." In the same tone, Grant wrote about Saxony: "God is now providing the means he will use later for the salvation of this land — Methodism."[51]

Both faith and fire had to be present for both the Bishop and the student to have such great expectations. In the complex tangle of cultures, languages, and religions that was Europe in 1905, the Methodists were probably hardly noticed. Europe's national and ethnic passions were even then moving toward August, 1914, and the war which demolished the easy optimism of the nineteenth century. Bishop Burt was a widely traveled cosmopolitan who had lived many years in Italy, had been decorated by the Italian King, had talked to heads of state, and had known the Hungarian patriot Kossuth. Grant Perkins was only a short while out of the primitive Kentucky mountains. Yet both shared the belief in the easy evangelical conquest of Europe. It was not to be.

Still, I believe that Bishop Burt understood Europe better

than did the Europeans themselves, trapped as they were in their own national and cultural boundaries and prejudices.

About Finland under Russian rule, Burt said, "Poor beautiful Finland under Russian rule, deprived of liberty. I confess I fell in love with Finland. On landing, every book, pamphlet, and paper in our luggage was examined by Russian officers. How free people are treated. But we (The Methodists) are now entering Russia through three doors — Finland, Germany and Bulgaria. We have a faithful group in St. Petersburg (now Leningrad). On one of our circuits in north Germany, the minister has two preaching stations in Russia. By paying a tax of about $500 he can secure the liberty to prosecute his work."

The Bishop also visited Hungary and Budapest on his way to his churches in Bulgaria. Hungary was then a part of the disintegrating Austrian Empire. He wrote, "Here we have a most interesting work. Since the revolution in 1848, Hungary has made great progress. There is religious liberty for all. Hence Jews are here in great numbers. The country reminds me of our central west with its immense farms and herds. Here is a coming nation which must be won for Christ."

Although Saxony was Protestant, it had established the Lutheran Church as a state church. Methodists were unwanted dissenters. Coming from the United States where the separation of church and state was an article of faith and a part of the Constitution, Grant was astonished.

He wrote: "When the writer inquired about the Methodist Church, a policeman gravely said it was no church but a chapel and the people no churchmen but dissenters."

And again: "There are persecutions here that one must think of Russia and not of Germany. At one place a Methodist member died, and the pastor of the established church forbade any funeral service. This was heeded except at the gravesite where a prayer was offered. The Methodist minister and the man in whose home the funeral took place were both fined 20 marks. At another place, prayer was forbidden in the Methodist chapel, only singing and speaking. But when the people came to the service they prayed silently. A policeman saw this and the preacher was fined 100 marks. Of course, there is no way of redress as the dissenters have no religious rights except those described."

Still, the Methodist Church as a free (not tax-supported) church was growing. Bishop Burt: "In Saxony where we suffered the most persecution, we are having the greatest success." At Plauen thousands came to hear him preach. Grant was there and wrote: "Methodism is reaching the young people of manufacturing Germany, putting sunshine in their hearts, joy on their faces, and songs on their lips. I have heard music before, but these young peoples' choruses can soon make one forget all but heaven."

Both the Bishop and the student were confident that democratic and religious freedom would save Europe. In 1906, universal suffrage had been pried out of the aging, pot-bellied monarchy of Austria-Hungary. That should have been salvation enough. Why, indeed, couldn't the hardy plant of democracy, so indigenous and native to the plains and mountains of America, be planted everywhere? We still have no answer to that question.

But even in 1905, Gavrilo Princip, a boy growing up in the mountains of Serbia, would show on June 28, 1914, how hollow such "progress" really was. It was he, putting two bullets into the body of Austrian Crown Prince Ferdinand at Serajevo, who triggered the unexpected chain reaction explosion that started World War I.

But all of that was unknown to Grant as he stood in a hall at Plauen, Saxony, in June, 1905, with over a thousand others and heard the beloved hymns of his church sung by a choir of young German workers. He was ecstatic and marching toward Zion.

Chapter Eighteen
The Passing Of The Alps

My father once told me that on his way from Germany to Rome in September, 1905, he had hiked through part of the Alps. While he lived I never pressed him for any details, an omission I now regret. But then the young are seldom sensitive to the magical moments in the lives of others, being so pre-occupied with their own.

An article he had published once, "The Passing Of The Alps", had to be the story of that journey; but I had no idea where to find it. Still, there might be one place where such an obscure item might be found — that vast curator of both the important and the unimportant — The Library of Congress.

After some time in the quiet stacks of that library where the religious periodicals are kept, the title snapped out at me from the pages of the March, 1909, issue of the *Methodist Review,* a small pocket size magazine of religious opinion.

It was the autumn of 1974. As I read the precious article sitting on the floor (there were no chairs or tables in the stacks), the important events of the day were roaring like wind through the nation and in the media. President Gerald Ford was explaining why he had pardoned former President Nixon. Judge Sirica was bludgeoning his way through the last of the Watergate trials. These were supposed to be the important affairs. But not to me. I was sharing my father's thoughts and feelings as he walked along the windy paths of the Alps so long ago.

Each article was signed by the facsimile signature of its

author. I had not seen that flowing signature for forty years, and I remembered how I had admired it and tried to copy it. It was an emotional moment of lucky discovery. It was as though he had just signed the article and was now going to tell me about a high moment in his life, even though I had never asked when he was alive.

The main theme of the article was surprising. It was a plea to save the Alps as a wilderness area before "the crowd has taken possession and the mob has appropriated them for its own. When these conditions grow worse, I join the pessimistic crowd and stand with those who weep the passing of the Alps."[52]

So he was an early environmentalist — an awkward word that we are probably stuck with. The grandchildren he never knew, including my two botanists, Vickey and Edwin, would have been proud of him. But not surprised if one remembers some important footnotes of American history.

In 1905, conservation was beginning to be a popular issue, pushed with "bully" vigor by President Theodore Roosevelt. At the begnning of his presidency he had made conservation an important part of his agenda. 148 million acres had been set aside as national forests, and over a million acres had been reserved for water power sites. Even then, America was starting to think about preserving rather than tearing up its resources.[53]

Grant began his walking tour through the Alps again with high expectations, but was met with "unsightly cogways ... barnlike hotels ... the barter of porters ... and the buzz of idle society."

He wrote sadly: "There is but one chain of Alps, and here those whom nature inspires drink their fill. But the hotel has become omnipresent. The tourists, sightseers, and loafers press closer and closer to the snows and the mosses, fill all the space, and turn the world upside down for first class."

"But there are a few places in this world too holy for the mob and too sacred for the money changers ... There are some things in life that cannot be had except at the expense of personal ease. The plunging cataracts and the somber gorge cannot be appreciated at a small cost. Thought and meditation, the prerequisites of the sublime, flourish best in the stillness of the rocks and under the power of the Alpine rose.

"The lightning express tourist might as well not visit the Alps as far as his personal good is concerned . . . Great impressions are not had on moving trains . . . The train goes on schedule. So does the stage. Even the mule has his own ideas and it is hard to divide time with him . . . When the cars keep moving, there is no time for absorption. The soul's windows remain closed . . . But here is nature's poise so grim, speaking in angry thunders but sometimes silent as death and incomprehensible as eternity."

He fell in with an old mountain guide who was being displaced by the railroads. "As I went over the barren rocks near Grimsel Pass, I overtook a bent man who reminded me of a pilgrim, worn and sad. He spoke of the things near his heart. How he loved the dizzy heights and everlasting white. Many a tale of adventure he had to tell (about) when he had led (others) up beyond the clouds to the summit of the monarch of the chain.

"But as I spoke of the projected cogway that was to cross the Pass near where we were standing, thus opening the crowd to the very center of the solitary and sublime, his spirits fell. In his youth he was the best guide in the Alps, reading the secrets of the elements with ease. He now earned his bread by keeping the loose stones out of the postway that had been cut from the mountain sides . . .

"As he paused for a moment before turning to his little cabin under the cleft just above us, a stage drawn by six horses dashed by. A woman, dressed in silks and buried in cushions looked listlessly out on the Alpine scene. A young man with kid-covered hands pointed with a smile at the grizzly mountaineer and the young student at his side. The crack of the driver's whip echoed back and forth from vale and crag. The old man turned. 'Yes, my day is past. There is no longer any room for me.'

"For a time I stood and looked at the fir tree cabin, and my heart went out to the old man whose life, home, and country had been invaded by the vulgarity of luxury."

Grant's feelings about the Alps were sometimes religious. "Here one has an experience like that of Moses when he stood on Sinai or of the ancient seers to whom God talked face to face. The soul that does not feel Omnipotence in those billowed convulsions is dead."

But more importantly, saving the wilderness and the sublime was necessary to save man. Grant closed the article in the rhetorical style so common in his times, but it comes through loud and clear as a splendid, almost poetical peroration. For the good of mankind, somehow there must be an end to the destruction of nature.

"If not this, how shall the race go when the forests, the mountains, and torrents shall be turned into commerce and bartered in the markets of the world? How shall live the prophets and seers when buyers and sellers shall fill the once awful solitude of gorge, mountain, steppe, and icy trail. Where shall dwell the sons of God when gold shall have destroyed the ideal and the dreamer is laughed to scorn. Will not the dews cease to fall and the rains refuse to water the earth? Will not the fountains be sealed and the world and all its bounties perish. When Niagara is no more and the great nature classics are destroyed — when the Alps are fallen — then the Gods must rear them high again . . . in order to teach us the ways of life again."

Chapter Nineteen

38 Via Firenze, Rome

When Grant walked out of the Alps at Geneva, Switzerland, he took a train for Rome, where he had been appointed as interim pastor of The American Methodist Church by Bishop Burt.

The autumn fields of Italy, tucked into neat squares by the hedgerows, were yellow and dry. The sun was high, the sky Italian blue. Just as Raphael would have painted it, Grant once wrote. Men, women, and children were everywhere in the fields, with high-wheeled carts bringing in the harvest. As the miles slipped by the windows of his second-class compartment, he let his mind slip by the centuries, pleasantly aware that he was entering an ancient and historic land.

Passengers entered and left his compartment as the train paused at flower-gardened stations. Friends and relatives, all talking furiously, saw new travelers, handing up hampers of food and bottles of wine for the journey. Then and now, Italians make a festive event of travel. At Rome in the big station, gray with train smoke, he took a horse cab to his destination, The Methodist Center at 38 Via Firenze at the corner of Via Venti Settembre

On the corner of two busy and historic streets, a short distance from the Quirinal (the residence of the King), he saw a large imposing five story structure. It housed The American Methodist Church (English speaking), The Italian Methodist Church, a book store, a publishing company for Italian church literature, offices, class rooms and a dormitory for a boy's school, as well as The Collegio Methodista to train young men in the ministry.

It had been built by The American Methodist Church in 1892 on the very street on which King Victor Emmanuel's soldiers, under Garibaldi, had marched into Rome to unify Italy on September 20, 1870. That was the significance of Via Venti Settembre. The Methodists did not hide their light under a basket.[54]

Encouraged by the religious toleration of Italy's new monarchy, the Methodists had arrived in Rome in 1874. Even so, their imposing headquarters in 1906 was out of proportion to their actual numbers in Italy then, reported by Bishop Burt in 1906 to be 2600.

But Grant began his new work enthusiastically. His was the English Church serving mostly travelers and Americans living in Rome. He visited the hotels, knew the American ambassador, and met a different kind of American than he had ever known well before, the rich cosmopolitan, the business man, the student, the diplomat, and the vactioneer, the kind of American in Rome once deftly painted by Henry James in his novel *Daisy Miller.*

He also met the young Italian ministerial students at the Methodista Collegio and practiced his faltering Italian on them. He probably also knew Miss Italia Garibaldi, the granddaughter of the savior of Italy, herself a Methodist and principal of the Methodist school for poor girls in another part of Rome.

He visited the Crandon School For Girls, founded and supported by the Women's Foreign Missionary Societies of the American church, a school so excellent that rich Roman families often sent their daughters there.

With his new friends, he watched Roman life from its sidewalk cafes, visited the old ruins of the Forum, walked the Appian Way, and viewed the Vatican and St. Peter's with mixed emotions. The magnificence of art and ancient tradition he saw told such a different story of Christianity than did the log church at Bear Creek Chapel on Meadowcreek. Even though God could comprehend both, the problem has always been that men could not.

Grant also studied at the American School of Classical Studies in Rome. I am not surprised. His was a sharply honed intellectual curiosity then. From the time he had eagerly read the new issues of *The Youth's Companion* as a boy, had been a teacher in a western army post, had dipped into Latin and geology at Union College, had immersed himself in biblical history at Drew, had sampled the excitement of Columbia University, and had tasted the medieval-modern mixture of Leipzig University, he had always taken pleasure in the use of his mind.

A combination of pride and Protestant militancy had led the American Methodist Episcopal Church to pour so much money and effort into its mission in Rome. It started about 1870 when the new Italian Monarchy approved of religious freedom. This would lead to some trouble later in 1910 when the obscure little church at 38 Via Firenze would be catapulted into world-wide western publicity by a half comic, half serious Catholic-Protestant hassle. Grant would write about this later.[55]

These Catholic-Protestant conflicts of the nineteenth century appear juvenile now, but perhaps the echoes of the Reformation sounded louder to the men of that day than they sound today.

At Rome he began to lay plans for a trip to the Holy Land, then under Turkish rule, that would be one of the emotional high points of his life.

13. The Methodist Center at 38 Via Firenza, Rome, in 1905
(Photo courtesy The United Methodist Church Archives
Lake Junaluska, North Carolina

Chapter Twenty
Pilgrimage

To all young ministers then, Palestine was The Holy Land and a pilgrimage there a high point in their lives. So, in February, 1906, Grant made plans for his visit there with two other ministers, Mr. Lytle of New Jersey and Mr. Keeler of Iowa. Through study and reading, he had developed and intensified his religious feelings, and so his joy at the prospect of walking on the same ground where Jesus walked was intense.

His diary is crammed with daily entries, sailing plans, schedules, and expenses. He also bought film for his camera. On February 13, he "left Rome at 10:45 A.M. after almost getting left. I did not have time to get my ticket so I handed the conductor fifteen lira with the promise of getting a ticket and change. He never showed up again.[56] I got through the station at Naples all right, and, after some hustling, went on board The Memfi, which sailed for Alexandria at 5:30 P.M."

It was five days and over one thousand kilometers to Alexandria on the Mediterranean. The fare was 146 francs. The Memfi was a graceful French ship with a long, pointed bowsprit like that of a sailing vessel. Again he was all glorious anticipation. "The sea is blue and my soul is full of glory."

In the morning mist and sunshine they sailed into Alexandria's harbor six days later. It was Sunday. They only had time to catch the morning train for Cairo, where they arrived at noon. From the omnipresent American Protestant Mission they got the names of several good "pensions" and struck a bargain at the Suisse, a small boarding hotel.

Americans tend to flock together wherever they are. That Sunday evening Grant "attended services at the American

Church where a good sermon was heard. I met several missionaries who had gathered from several places in Egypt for their annual conference and new appointments." Egypt was then under English rule.

Monday, February 19. "It was agreed last night to go to the Pyramids today. We took the train to Bedrasheen where we got donkeys for the entire day. First, we saw the site of Old Memphis, beautiful dwelling. After, we crossed the valley and began to ascend to the desert. Looking back, how beautiful the green valley of the Nile and how significant the line where sand and grass meet."

Sixty-three years later, in 1969, I first saw the Nile's green ribbon from a height of thirty thousand feet. From Athens, we had passed Crete and had come to the north African landfall on our way to Uganda, where our son Edwin was in the Peace Corps. It was a spectacular line where the intense blue of the sea meets the intense white of the desert. I could see the prehistoric vestiges of river valleys that had lost their waters.

Later, near Khartoum in The Sudan, the pilot pointed out the Nile, a slim finger of blue and green in the white waste, so delicately poised between life and oblivion. My father on a donkey in 1906 and I in a jet plane in 1969, both with the same thought: "How significant the line where sand and grass meet."

After a two-hour ride Grant and his friends arrived at Gizeh and the silent monolithic pyramids that have so fascinated men. Here he took two pictures. He wrote: "This has been a red letter day in my travels. I shall never expect another like it." Later, just before they left Egypt he went back by himself. "I took a train again for the Pyramids. After rambling around those mysteries, I took a seat on the rear platform of the car and enjoyed the most glorious sunset I have ever seen. The Pyramids grew less in size as we sped away from them. Night came on and stars lit up the sky. The Pyramids sank into a gloom as black as the history that surrounds them. I bid goodbye to some friends at the mission and went to my room to meditate on the things of the day."

In Cairo he visited a Moslem school. "Here four thousand or so students learn to recite The Koran and something of the Tenets of the Great Prophet. They sit in groups, eating, talking, reading and constantly swaying. I thought, this will not stand the test of the twentieth century."

He confidently expected that Islam would lose its force "when translated into virile and progressive English". He lived at the crest of the missionary movement at the start of this century. I write at its end. We are all provincial to our times, and so I can hardly blame him that he did not foresee Islam today, the fastest growing religion in some parts of the world and the start of its oriental roots among American Blacks.

But it was time to say goodbye to Egypt, when they left Cairo by train and arrived at Port Said at noon, February 21. There at the northern end of the Suez Canal they boarded a Russian steamer bound for Jaffa. "Finding all the first and second class cabins taken, we took third class and decided to sleep on deck. The ship had considerable motion, and we did not regret the good suppers served in the first and second class cabins. After declaring we were glad to be alive, we spread our blankets on the deck and lay down to pleasant dreams."

The next morning they arrived off the coast at Jaffa, now Tel Aviv. But the seas were heavy and they could not land. Then, without any port facilities, passengers and freight at Jaffa had to be taken off in lighters and small boats, useless in heavy weather.

Grant wrote: "Hour after hour the sea rose, and the ship bobbed up and down. I had my first case of real sea-sickness. We had nothing to do but wait. At seven in the evening the ship weighed anchor and put to sea for Beirut. Mr. Keeler and I got our supper in the second class cabin. After some time, I went to sleep on the deck again to dream of the comforts of home and the joys of heaven."

What was it like to spend two nights on the deck of a Russian coastal ship in the eastern Mediterranean? Edwin, the grandson Grant never knew, had a similar experience on Lake Malawi in Africa, visiting an African friend while in The Peace Corps. He described that scene to us in a letter in 1969.

"The rest of the trip was up the lake by boat. First class was too expensive, and so we got the cheap class. Really bad conditions, people living all over the floor. But we sneaked up to the forward prow and spent most of the trip among all the ropes and anchors, wind-blown and sun-burned. It was really neat. There were several volunteers from other countries. I really felt a sense of unity among them. We were the new breed of whites, unlike the colonists, going third class."

To Grant the trip to Beirut was unexpected, like being flown to Washington when bad weather shuts in New York. He wrote: "This morning we were put off at Beirut and found ourselves at the Victoria Hotel, not too late for a good breakfast. After getting the kinks out, we had dinner and drove to the Dog River where we saw the old road, the war path of the nations in ancient times which crosses a bold promentory extending out into the sea.

"As I stood there I cannot describe my feelings. Behind us were the snow-capped Lebanons. The pressure of the sea had bored out great caves at the water's edge. The force sent up geysers, a picture of great beauty. The grooves of countless chariots are in the stone. I could almost hear the grind of the wheels and the cries of the officers driving their men on."

Under Turkish rule, Christians and Moslems seemed to live in harmony in Beirut. He wrote Saturday, February 24, 1906. "Today has been a glorious day. We have nothing to do except read, think, and enjoy the glories around us. We have a good hotel, fine service, good food, and pleasant people. During the afternoon, Mr. Gillman of the American Press and I walked out to the Syrian Protestant College, a college with a magnificent plant and over seven hundred students. Truly, light is shining in this land."

After three days and another coastal ship, they "were pulling for the shore at Haifa one mile away to run the gauntlet of Turkish customs." At last he was in the Holy Land of his dreams.

*14. The steamer Memfi in Messina Harbor, February 1906, on its way to Alexandria
(Photo by Grant Perkins)*

Chapter Twenty-One
In The Holy Land

Four oarsmen pulled the cluttered lighter through the clear waters off Haifa. The olive trees and white houses on Mount Carmel were clean and bright in the morning sun. At last he was in the land of Jesus and his beloved Bible, peopled with Old Testament prophets and New Testament saints.

But before the Bible there was a hotel and breakfast. From the number of times he mentioned in his diary these comforts of travel, I know he had the robust appetite of a young man, unimpaired by ulcers and unafraid of strange food.

On February 26. "The morning was glorious as we walked up the winding road through the German colony along the mountainside to the crest of Carmel. Here we enjoyed a magnificent view. To the west the blue Mediterranean. To the north Acre, Sidon, and the Lebanon Mountains. Turning we could see the ranges of Galilee and the Plain of Esdraelon."

They took a horse carriage for Nazareth, a trip of about twenty-four miles that took several hours over a rough stone-packed road. Beyond Nazareth it was only another twenty-five miles to the eastern boundary at the Sea of Galilee, lying below the Golan Mountains. Israel today is tightly squeezed between mountain and sea. One can understand her fierce determination now not to let an unrelenting Syrian enemy back on the Golan Heights without a peace.

After leaving the Carmel ridge of hills and crossing the Kishon River, they came to the Plain of Esdraelon, the valley of Megiddo in biblical times, the fertile remains of a dried up swamp. Soon they were going up the hills of Nazareth.

"We began the ascent of the hills, covered with olive

groves, dark and red and white anemones. Distant Mount Tabor came into full view. The mountains of Samaria were to the right. The road was narrow, muddy with spring rains, with very sharp turns." A friend has told me that even today you can only make a turn on some roads near Nazareth by backing your car first into the side of the hill.

Suddenly Nazareth came into view. "I cannot describe my feelings as we entered the village, the scene of the boyhood of Him whom I rejoice to know as Friend and God." But except for Mary's well, he was not impressed with such tourist attractions as Joseph's workshop. That evening he sat for a while by the well and then wrote the following sensitive passage.

"No bunglesome art can give back to the world those places so closely associated with the life of Our Lord. But since the well has been the place for the common supply of water from immemorial time, and there is no other, the Virgin Mother must have brought her child as she drew water for the needs of her family. For some time I watched the women, girls, and children come in scores, fill their vessels, and bear them away on their heads.

"Some were old. Some were middle aged but bore traces of hard toil. Some were girls, happy and gay. Some were children with laughing eyes. As I turned from this place, I could only think that He whose teachings have lifted women from slavery carried water for his mother. Wherever His Gospel is known, women's burdens have become lighter."

The next morning he got up early to see the sun rise over Nazareth and then took a carriage for Tiberias on the Sea of Galilee, now Lake Kinneret. They passed the village of Remeh, now the Christian village of Reina in Israel. Then Cana, where Jesus turned the water into wine, now Kafr Kanna, an Arab village in Israel where pomegranates are grown. They were poverty-plagued villages then and not bustling and prosperous as today. From there it was all downhill, for Lake Kinneret is 680 feet below sea level.

He wrote about seeing Galilee for the first time. "As we slowly went down the winding way to the village of Tiberias, the beauty, stillness, and lovely solitude of this sea where Jesus loved so much to be, shall never be forgotten."

That evening they hired a fishing boat for a sail on Lake Galilee. The sun went down behind Mount Tabor as the high prow cut through the quiet evening waters. Because of the depressed elevation, it was warmer than in the highlands.

Tiberias was then a squalid village, its narrow streets carrying both traffic and sewage. Only three years before in 1903, a cholera epidemic had killed many people there. Built by Herod Antipas when Jesus was twenty-two, it was named after the Roman Emperor then.

The Gospels and history had filled the borders of this lake with prosperous towns, a vital people, and the pillars of Rome. He found it empty. He wrote about his feelings that night. "Around this sea the greater part of my Lord's ministry was accomplished. The prosperous cities to which he preached, the throbbing life in which he moved have all passed away. Nothing but desolation remains."

The next morning they were up at sunrise to sail to the northern end of the lake to see the ruins of Capernaum. The lake was calm that day; but when the hot winds came out of the east, it could be very turbulent and dangerous.

They were back in Tiberias by noon, so small is this sea. At the little hotel they ate fish just caught out of the lake. (Tiberias is now a winter resort in Israel, clean, modern, and filled with good hotels for winter vacationers, quite different from the empty shores that Grant saw. But one feature of its restaurants still is fish just caught from Lake Kinneret.) By evening they were back in Nazareth.

Chapter Twenty-Two

On Horseback to Jerusalem

Thursday, March 1st. Almost seventy miles south of Nazareth lay Jerusalem. Across those miles there was then no road or railroad. So there was only one way to go — on horseback.

Grant and his two friends hired horses and bought provisions for the three day trip. Grant, the former cavalryman, looked over the horses first. They were ugly and gaunt-sided, not likely to win any prizes. But he knew the ponies of the Sioux Indians looked the same way and yet were tough prairie travelers. The dragoman, or local travel agent, said that the horses could be left at their destination, as one would leave a rental car.

Grant wrote: "At nine this morning we found ourselves in the saddle for the journey to Jerusalem. We came out of Nazareth, turned to the left over rough hills down to the Plain of Esdraelon, sixty years ago lying waste but now somewhat cultivated. We saw natives following the plow one by one as in the days of Elijah."

The hills of Nazareth were really the foothills of the Lebanon Mountains. The plain or valley was the dividing line between the Old Testament kingdoms of Judea and Israel. His thoughts that morning were a rich tapestry of Old Testament pageantry from his name and place-studded Bible, his own intense scholarship, and his feelings at seeing these scenes at last.

By 1905 agriculture was having a new start under the fellaheen or farmer and new Jewish immigrant communities. The first morning they had to get used to their horses, but soon found that their plodding mounts knew how to pick their way over the barren and stone-pocked road, a road marked by forty centuries of wear.

They stopped for lunch near Shumian, a town made famous by Elisha who raised the child of the Shumanite woman. It is now the village of Solem, close by the present West Bank cities of Merhavya and Afula. Of course, Grant never saw Afula, which was only founded in 1925 by The Jewish American Commonwealth.

They climbed the slopes of Little Hermin, 1690 feet. "It was a hard climb but the view fully repaid all of our efforts. Dozens of cities could be pointed out. With a long and lingering look I turned from the spot and came down to more real life and rode south."

Later, "we passed Jezreel, the royal city of Ahab, but there is nothing but squalor and dirt here now. Poor people. The women and children seem to do all the work while the men sit around and smoke." It began to rain and they made themselves as comfortable as possible in rubber ponchos.

"Pushing through the mud, we were glad when, at 5:30 PM, we reached our stopping place, Jemin, for the night." They had ridden almost twenty miles. Dunning, an enterprising American tourist guide then, tells about Jemin, then a Turkish garrison town.

"As usual, an official came to inspect the passports (of Dunning's party). What he really wants is baksheesh. Let that be forthcoming and the correctness of the documents is a minor matter."[57] Since Grant does not mention the subject in his diary, it is likely that the Turkish officer thought three wet and dirty young Americans not worth much baksheesh.

Dunning was then conducting large tours by encampment. He would take large parties through Palestine furnishing tents, food, and equipment. If one really wanted to go first class, he could ride in a sedan chair covered with pillows between two mules. Dunning would send equipment ahead so that the tourist would find the tents up and supper cooking when he rode in.

Dunning described his operation. "Our camp is a small city. We have sixteen sleeping tents, two large saloon tents, and a kitchen tent. The sleeping tents are furnished with cot beds, tables, and rugs, equal in comfort to any hotel."[58]

Friday, March 2. Grant wrote: "Early, we mounted our ponies and crossed some rocky hills. After an hour, we dismounted and had breakfast on a large stone by the side of the road. There are signs of industry, and the country is well watered. Sometimes we heard the shepherd's rustic music reed, resembling the music of a Scottish bag pipe. We have been on the great caravan road of old, the highway of the nations which passes through Dothan. Dothan is a lovely basin, rich in water supply and pasture land." He was at the ruins now called Tel Dothan.

Alone in the March sunshine where a large spring flows out of the tel or hill, Grant saw the people of his Bible. How perfectly, he thought, the place fitted the stories. Jacob had sent his sons with his flocks from Hebron in Judea below Jerusalem to look for pasture. They had gone to the Vale of Dothan. Later, Jacob had sent his favorite son Joseph to find them. His brothers hated Joseph, "the dreamer", with his new coat so they sold him into slavery. (Genesis 37:12 to 29) And this was the very valley of the story.

When Grant's party left the Vale of Dothan, they started up the hills of Samaria, eventually reaching the Roman garrison town of Sebastia. "We could see traces of Rome on all sides, the Greek theatre at the foot, the Forum Sebastia, and, on top, the colonnade of Herod's Palace. And buried beneath the ruins Ahab's City on a Green Hill, the capital of the ten tribes, its glory past."

Finally, that day they came to Nablus, the Shechem of Old Testament days, a green oasis between two mountains, Ebald and Gerizim, and today daily in the news in the grim struggle between Arab and Jew. It was a larger city, close-packed with narrow streets, gray with stone walls from which rose the graceful reeds of Moslem minarets. They stayed at the Roman Catholic Convent that night, after a ride of about twenty-five miles.

Saturday March 3. "This morning Mr. Lytle and I were up with the sun on Mount Gerizim. We first stood on Jothan's pulpit, and then to the top of the mountain where we found about one hundred sixty survivors of the Samaritan sect and the ruins of an old temple. It was a longer walk than we had thought and we were about famished when we reached the Latin Convent for our breakfast."

Here on this mountain that Moses had seen across the Jordan Valley, the Samaritans had been practicing the same religious rites for 2500 years. They were disturbed sometimes by young toughs from Nablus come to jeer at these strange relicts. They still exist today in modern Israel.

You cannot live with a horse for three days without growing fond of him. Theirs were independent creatures, finding their own way, water, and forage. At least two of them were no longer nameless, a sure sign that they were now accepted into this little body of the family of man.

"As morning passed, we pushed our ponies, Eleazar and Tomite, through a country highly cultivated but without much water. Turning from the main road, we reached Shiloh for lunch. There is nothing here but barren waste and a few ruins." In that silent place, the voice of Jeremiah was heard in his Bible. "But go ye now to my place which was in Shiloh ... and see what I did to it for the wickedness of my people Israel." (Jeremiah 7:12)

Near Bethel, now Beitem, they first saw Jerusalem, clear but distant fifteen miles away in the late afternoon sunshine. "At last we came to the top of a mountain. In front we could see Jerusalem. As I looked on this city, strong emotions filled me. I stopped the others and offered a prayer of thanksgiving. We spurred our horses and were not long in reaching our hotel at Ramullah where a fine dinner awaited us. Here we parted from our faithful horses as we expect to go to Jerusalem in the morning by carriage."

Ramullah, high in the hills, was cool in the summer, even in 1906, a place where people from Jerusalem would come to escape the summer heat. They had ridden again over twenty miles. Because he had been out of the saddle since 1898, not surprisingly, he wrote, "We are sore, tanned, and disfigured, but glad we have made the journey through the land once so favored by God and now a silent witness of His vengeance for its sins."

How different was Grant's tour from those of today. He climbed mountains, was wet by the rain, slept in simple guest houses, sat alone by ancient wells as his horse grazed the grasses of immemorial valleys, and he had time to meditate what he saw and felt.

15. Jerusalem inside the Damascus Gate
(Photo by Grant Perkins, March, 1906)

16. A Bedouin tent on the road to Jericho
(Photo by Grant Perkins, March, 1906)

17. Boys in the Kidron Valley, February, 1906
(Photo by Grant Perkins)

Chapter Twenty-Three

Jerusalem

Sunday, March 4. "This morning after a good night's rest we drove into Jerusalem. The morning was perfect as we sped rapidly along the new carriage road. About 10 AM we rounded the top of the hill and there was Jerusalem full before us."

There is even now no city like Jerusalem in all the world. It is the root from which three world religions grew. There the Prophet Mohammed went to Heaven from the Temple Rock. There the Jews pray at the Wailing Wall. There Jesus was crucified on a hill called Golgotha. These people and religions share a common God, but are so estranged that we hold our breaths that this tiny slice of land and passions might be the trigger that pushes us all into a final Armageddon.

Grant saw a city of about sixty thousand. Moslems were the ruling aristocracy, even though in a minority. The Jews, who had been coming back to the city of their fathers for some time, were in the majority. The number of Christians was in between. The Moslems were not then fanatical, only a little contemptuous of the lowly Jews and the quarreling Christians.

Grant went at once to the Mount of Olives, going out Saint Stephens gate. He sat for a while taking in the city. The hill was cluttered with shrines and churches. When he had heard the scriptures read as a boy in Bear Creek Chapel, he saw the Mount of Olives as like the green Kentucky hills. Now he wrote, "As I left the Mount and re-crossed the Kidron, I longed to see it as it was in our Saviour's time, no walls, no cumbersome buildings, but covered with olive trees."

The next day he spent "investing the walls" of the city.

It was a day long walk, beginning early in the morning out the Jaffa Gate. "The scene is very beautiful. Camels, donkeys, wagons, and carriages were moving here and there."

Tuesday, March 6. In the rain they set out for Jericho by carriage. "The clouds were lowering as we passed out of St. Stephen's Gate over the Kidron to Bethany on the other side of the Mount of Olives. This squalid village, whose inhabitants are the most importunate beggars I ever saw, has nothing of interest now." No hint of those two delightful women, Mary and Martha, whom Jesus had met there.

The road to Jericho was muddy and rough. Some years before 1906, thieves hiding in the rugged hills had often robbed the pilgrims. The Turkish government had solved the problem by hiring a local tribe of Bedouins to ride escort or "shotgun". Dunning reports that they still did so by 1912, even though the trip was no longer considered dangerous.[59]

Looking west from the Mount of Olives Grant was vaguely aware of a deep hole in the earth. As they went toward Jericho, always downward, the air became heavier and his feeling of plunging into a hole increased. It was true. From a height of about 1800 feet above sea level at Jerusalem, they finally reached tha level of the Dead Sea at about 1290 feet below sea level. The high pressure of the air would run the mercury of a pocket barometer off the scale and ruin it. This was a drop of 3000 feet in less than 20 miles. And still, the bottom of the Dead Sea is an unfathomable 2500 feet below its surface.[60]

"After dinner (at Jericho) we set out for the Jordan River six miles distant, passing several Bedouin Camps." There Grant took pictures of ragged Bedouin boys. He found the Jordan "a very insignificant river". He thought how much more beautiful was the green cool passage of the Cumberland River over the rocks and falls in Kentucky. They drove through the thick mud of the estuary to the Dead Sea. Its lifeless silence was immense and its waters an unnatural blue-green. There was no bathhouse, but the men went to the right and the women to the left to prepare to go into the water.

Thursday, March 8. After another day in Jerusalem, they drove south about six miles to Bethlehem where the beauty of the Christmas story was almost destroyed for Grant by what he saw.

"Here was a scene which took away all feelings of reverence for the place where Christ was born. It now contains three basilicas, the Greek, Armenian, and Latin, each taking alternate hours for their services. Their hatred and animosity are so great and they guard their times and places with such zeal, that often general fights and knockdowns occur in spite of the Turkish soldiers who always must stand guard to keep the peace."

But Golgotha, the low hill outside the Damascus Gate where Jesus was said to have been crucified, was denied Grant. It was then a walled Turkish cemetery. But it had not always been denied the Christians.

As Dunning tells it, "The hill, a cemetery, was also a place where Moslem women came to sit in the open air and chat with other ladies. Religious services (of the Christians) with preaching and singing could not fail to disturb them. They might have endured this but visitors were often rude. Moslem women are heavily veiled. So many . . . forgot . . . common courtesy. They pushed and jostled the women to see through their veils. When the Moslems heard that a Sunday School Convention was coming, they refused admittance to all Christians."[61]

But Grant's feelings toward this place were only matched by his determination to see it. "I climbed to the top of the big Latin building just outside the Damascus Gate, now in the course of construction. As it is now a Moslem cemetery and no one is allowed in, I went to the rock cliff on the east side of the Grotto, climbed up the precipice, and found myself on the top of Calvary. I saw a Moslem guard lying behind a tomb, but apparently asleep, as I passed within ten paces of him. Crossing to the other side, I found the wall too high and steep to scale. But in another part I found no trouble an springing over a wall to the olive orchard below." He had been a trespasser on Golgotha.

Saturday, March 10. Grant noted his 33rd birthday. Early in the morning he saw Mr. Keeler and Mr. Lytle off for Jaffa at the little train station outside Jerusalem.

Treves described this station in *The Land That Was Lost* thus: "As for the station itself, it is a small house enclosed in a fence. Outside the fence are the hotel touts, the cab runners, bazaar scouts, shopmen's pickets, and guides. To this rabble the defenseless tourist is flung as a sheep to the wolves."[62]

Sunday, March 11. He went to the Church of the Sepulcher where "I heard a medley of passionate confusion. The Coptic and Armenian services were going on at the same time. Going to another level there was still another. All about were Turkish soldiers, with stacked guns, ready to keep the peace. I think the Moslem is a superior being as far as his religious life is concerned. He will never be converted to Christianity, and with good reason, until he is put in touch with a better life than he now sees."

For the third time Grant went to the Mount of Olives, and walked from Bethany to the Mount, just as Jesus had done when he had "wept over the city". He wrote: "After spending about two hours on the Mount of Olives under a large olive tree reading the New Testament, I returned to the hotel." He closed his Bible at Luke 19 and looked about this memory drenched slope for the last time.

He left Jerusalem by train Monday morning, March 12, for Jaffa where he boarded a Russian steamer at 5:30 PM for Port Said. From Port Said the next morning, he went by train to Alexandria the same evening. On March 14th, he visited the American warship Brooklyn, and then went on board a Greek passenger-freighter for Pireaus.(I am impressed by how well developed public transportation was.)

He was enchanted with Greece where after a visit of several days, he took a train to Patras on the west coast to board a ship bound for Brindisi on the heel of Italy. His trip was ending, but something was missing. Not once did he mention those modern paranoic impediments to modern travel — the passport and the visa. Not in Holland, Germany, Italy, or Turkey. In those days you simply did not need them.

While I was with him, writing about his trip to Palestine, all that I had ever read about that land blended into his feelings about it. He and Israel have become very real to me. This ancient, significant land moved and stimulated him, often to pure joy. On Sunday, March 18, on the Adriatic Sea, he said a lovely goodbye.

"The morning dawned bright and fair on the Adriatic. The world seems full of light, warmth, and life. This is a Sabbath in which I can worship God in a way I can be nearest to Him. As we go up the coast, beautiful islands are everywhere seen. About 10 we came to the island of Corfu. I went ashore and took a long walk gathering wild flowers. Beauty everywhere. At 5 we sailed away up the Sound and from that to dark every moment had some new surprise of beauty.

"This is my last day at sea for a while. I am glad and sad. Glad that my tour is over and I can get back to work. Sad that I am leaving behind, perhaps forever, with such a superficial knowledge, those lands about which it has ever been my delight to read and of which I have struggled hard to know — Egypt, Palestine, and Greece.

"But I am thankful for blessings received and for aspirations realized, and shall set my foot on land tomorrow with a grateful heart and in a degree satisfied."

18. Camel outside the Jaffa Gate, Jerusalem, 1906
(Photo by Grant Perkins)

121

19. Mount of Olives from the bridge, 1906
(Photo by Grant Perkins)

20. The Damascus Gate, Jerusalem, 1906

21. The Via Dolorosa, Jerusalem, 1906

Chapter Twenty-Four
Bachelor Minister

The ship Romanic arrived in Boston from Naples, Italy, on July 4, 1906.[63] Grant, anxious to see America again, was among its passengers. His diary now silent, he felt none of the excitement he had felt going over in 1905. But I do have a scrap of his verse that describes his feelings as he came into Boston harbor.

Oh for news that I can read.
Oh for a meal of American food.
Oh for a tongue that I can speak.
Oh for the sight of a friendly face.
Oh to talk to an American girl.
Oh for a bit of American grace.

His homecoming feelings were intensified by his disappointments. About his return he wrote once: "As our ship dropped anchor in Boston harbor, I breathed the fresh air of America again. And what a change. It was like coming from prison to freedom. When I read on the door of the Governor's office at the capitol, 'Walk in', I almost fainted. Imagine seeing such a sign on the door of any official in Germany. I had gone, seen, and tasted, and that was enough."

That day Boston was full of firecrackers, oratory, and parades. But he did see two friendly faces as he came ashore. His cousin, James Faulkner, who had been his college president at Union, and Will Harris, his classmate. They were both then in graduate school at Harvard. Seeing them, memories flooded him, memories of his home in the green mountains of Kentucky and of his days in the little college there.

They all went to Faulkner's home in Cambridge where they talked far into the night about Grant's stories of Europe. That summer Grant had a scholarship at Harvard Divinity School and took a course under the famous American psychologist, William James.

After a delightful summer at Harvard, he began to think restlessly about the rest of his life. He was thirty-three and time was getting late. "A place on the faculty and as vice president of a small mid-western college was offered me just after I had left Harvard. But my ideal of a minister was as a pastor, and I did not feel that this would answer my mother's dying prayer." The power of her memory was very strong, but I believe now he was always essentially a scholar, loving the use of his mind and intellect. In later years I believe he may have regretted this first decision. At any rate, he came to the Conference of the Kentucky Methodist Church North at Greenup in September, 1906, and agreed to go to the church at Latonia, Kentucky, now a part of Covington. Salary was $800 a year and house.

But first he had promised to be guest preacher at Trinity Methodist Church at Louisville, Kentucky.[64] In high spirits he took the train from Greenup. Fresh in his mind were the fervent words of the Bishop, the lively debate about Conference resolutions, the hymns still ringing in his ears, and the camaraderie with other believers in Christ, Methodist style, and his appointment at last to his own church.

After an all night train ride, he arrived Sunday morning at Trinity Church, where he was met by a slender black-haired girl of nineteen who introduced herself as the organist. Together, they chose the hymns to be sung. As young as she was, Victorine McDaniel was already known as a concert organist.

Trinity Church was only half full this September morning, as is often true when the parishioners know there is an unknown substitute in the pulpit. Grant allowed himself a few discreet but not entirely ministerial glances at Victorine's slender figure as she played. After the services, she introduced him to her father, John McDaniel, a tall, bluff man with handle-bar moustache. He had a photographic studio in downtown Louisville and did mug shots for the Louisville Police Department.

Grant went to their home for dinner and was entertained until evening. The treasurer of Trinity Church had given him fifteen dollars for his services in supplying the pulpit. As he walked to the Louisville Hotel in the soft September evening, he felt a glow. He had money in his pocket. He had just spent a pleasant day with a very pretty girl. And tomorrow he was going to his own church to begin his career at the age of thirty-three. There are few better moments in life.

At Latonia, he once wrote: "My field was around the famous track, and the church was a little frame building which had begun as an Episcopal Mission."

He worked hard on his sermons, and visited all of his members. He typed the bulletins, helped the finance chairman see that all the bills were paid, recruited Sunday school teachers, had the piano tuned, mediated a dispute between two church officials, gave lantern slide lectures of his pictures of his travels to his members (who were proud to have such a well traveled young man as their minister), looked into the shining eyes of young parents as he baptized their first child, and held tight the sobbing man whose wife had just died.

Soon he felt the inadequacy of the little frame church. It was only heated by a smoky pot-bellied stove. Later, after the new church was built, it was ignominiously moved a block away to become a movie theatre. "I began at once to dream dreams. Within six months I had persuaded an architect to visualize those dreams. Within another few months we had ten thousand dollars in cash and some subscriptions for a new church."[65]

But now for the first time, he learned that the ministry is made up of two equal parts — the Grace of God and the perversity of men. As his happy plans matured, he was not aware that one silent opponent had the ear of his District Superintendent, his superior officer in the Methodist scheme of things.

He wrote: "I had not thought of a change (of churches) until my District Superintendent, answering my direct question, told me frankly it looked like a move, because the consensus of the people was that I had been too aggressive."

This news stunned Grant. Of course he knew about the doubters who never want anything changed in a church, but they were not known to him. He invoked the congregational vote on his return. Seventy-three voted for his return and three against.

He had beaten City Hall; but because he had twisted the ecclesiastical tail, he may also have endangered his career. After all, among the Methodists then, only Bishops and District Superintendents decided about appointments, not congregations and ministers.

About the aftermath, Grant wrote: "My D. S. (as that officer was called) was a good man, his family attended my church, and we never disagreed except at the time I invoked the congregational vote. He told me that was not Methodistic, and had it not been for the nearly unanimous vote, he would have removed me. I never did hear of the consensus of opinion after that. Just one man had conviced the D. S. that my program could not be realized and things would go smash if pushed through."

In Latonia he lived in only a couple rooms of the commodious parsonage as bachelors generally live — untidily. His roll top desk with its brass lamp and green glass shade, was the most imposing piece of furniture in the house. A worn leather Morris chair, discarded by a former minister, a few other pieces of furniture, and his books, made up his quarters. There was an iron cook stove, fired with wood, and a few pots and pans.

Cooking was never one of his accomplishments, and I can never remember when I was a boy that he ever took much interest in the kitchen. But mealtime at home was always white tableclothes and napkins, and hot bowls lined up beside the empty plates. He would fill our plates leisurely, sometimes too slowly for me. Mealtime was also a time for conversation and important news.

I remember two news items very clearly. I can remember the sadness on his face on January 7, 1919, when he announced that his Spanish War friend, Teddy Roosevelt, had died. And on a rainy day in November, 1916, he told us exultantly that Michigan had voted dry, for Prohibition was his one political passion and hope. My younger brother Jack got a laugh asking, how could that be, it was raining outside.

So I am certain that he prepared meals at Latonia only out of necessity and eagerly accepted every invitation to dine with a member of his church.

He had lived more or less contentedly in army barracks in South Dakota and Nebraska, in a student's room at Union College, in room 301 in Hoyt-Browne Hall at Drew Seminary, in a boarding house of an insufferable German landlady at Leipzig, and on a noisy Roman street. But he was chasing adventure and the holy grail of knowledge then. With such companions he wasn't lonely.

But Grant was now vaguely lonely and restless in his rooms, and the name and figure that kept rising in his mind was that of the slender girl in Louisville, playing the organ so gracefully.

128

22. and 23. Trinity Methodist Church
Latonia, (now a part of Covington) Kentucky
Grant's first church after his return from Europe in 1906

Chapter Twenty-Five

Victorine

One day in September, 1907, Victorine McDaniel opened a letter from Latonia. Other letters had come from Grant that year, chatty but of no real significance. Now he said he was coming to the Methodist Conference at Louisville and wanted to call. Her instincts told her that this letter was different.

A little apprehensive and curious as are all mothers of twenty-year-old daughters, her mother asked from whom the letter came. "From Mr. Perkins. He wants to see me." Victorine remembered the evening a year before when he had told her about ships at sea, walking through the Alps, and riding a horse over the hills of Palestine. She had tingled with pleasure at his voice telling his adventures.

She lived in a bustling and lively family of three younger sisters and two brothers. They had all been sad at the death of her oldest sister Loni in 1906. But her younger sisters, Martha and Dedie, gayly pestered her about the not so young man who had singled her out for a visit.

From scraps of poems written earlier, I know that Grant had other skirmishes with love. There was one about a withered rose and another about a ring returned. Because young men always write about love in the particular and not in the abstract, I feel certain that these poems were not simply exercises in a poetry class.

Victorine was a lovely girl, large dark eyes, long dark-brown hair swept up high on her head, and a slight private smile passing over the slim grecian oval of her face. She had musical talent, and a subtle reserve, and was making a precarious living as a music teacher.

She had liked him, even though amused at his baldness. At thirty four he was middle-aged by post-Victorian standards. He was always sensitive about being bald. He once told me that he began losing his hair in the Spanish War after malarial bouts. He spoke of it as though being bald was a moral fault that needed an excuse. So, sometime he got a hair piece or toupee as they were then called.

When my brother Jack and I were small boys and we saw him early in the morning without his toupee, the sight would break us up. But the Turkish red fez or hat with a tassle that he had brought back from his travels was often a useful substitute for his toupee indoors at home. But I am sure that when he called at the McDaniel residence in September, 1907, he had not yet given in to hirsute deceit, but bore his embarrassment stoically.

He once wrote me about the principal events in his life. "The next year, the courtship started during Conference. We were married December 26, 1907." Apparently he had taken little action after they had met in 1906. I could have been very annoyed with him. Was he going to let this lovely creature slip away? Didn't he know that such a lovely peach would not remain long unplucked? But I will have to say this for him. Once started, he wasted no time. In those days, three months between the first tentative ritual of courtship and marriage was, as they would say among the racing touts at Latonia, a fast track.

A minister at a church conference must necessarily be in church. So I am sure that Grant and Victorine went somewhere first together to church, his fellow ministers looking approvingly at their bachelor friend's pretty companion. They sat together in the pew, trying to get away from the crowd. Grant was intensely aware of her person, her brown eyes, the enchanting curve of her neck, the starchy white folds of her dress, and her long fingers. Their hands touched and closed in intimate privacy as they sat close together.

They only half listened to the sermon. There were other messages for them, and the young of every generation hear their beautiful sounds, always they believe for the first time in history.

After the Conference in Louisville, Grant brought back two

pieces of news to his little congregation of two hundred at Latonia — that he would be coming back as their minister and that in December he would be bringing a wife back also.

Not even their proposed new church was as exciting as the latter news. It was probably an important topic of conversation at the meeting of the Women's Foreign Missionary Society, around dinner tables of the congregation, and after church. Who was she? What was her name? Some eyebrows were raised at the news that she was only twenty. Why (wistfully) didn't he choose one of the unmarried girls in the congregation. I am sure a good time was had by all. It is not often that a small congregation of church people can engage in the delicious pastime of sizing up or of approving or even disapproving the new wife of their bachelor minister.

After their marriage in Louisville, Kentucky, the day after Christmas in 1907, there was no honeymoon. On eight hundred dollars a year, there are no Caribbean cruises. Victorine faced the inevitable church reception for her with a little apprehension. She felt and was so young. But she need not have worried. The men especially universally acclaimed her and congratulated her smiling husband. For Grant, even his winter days were all sunshine.

24. Victorine McDaniel Perkins, 1907

Chapter Twenty-Six
Moving to Michigan

After two years at Latonia, a friend who had become the District Superintendent of the church in Detroit asked Grant to join him there. Grant sensed that the inevitable move was coming anyhow and accepted. In those days the Methodists moved their preachers around as though they were IBM assistant managers. The system of the itinerant preacher who preached and moved on, a relic of pioneer days, took a long time to die in Methodist tradition.

So they left Latonia in the late summer of 1909. Victorine, expecting her first baby in November, went home to Louisville. Grant went north to Detroit, where the Bishop appointed him to the church at Onaway, Michigan, high up in the north part of the southern peninsula.

Even though Michigan had been admitted as a state in 1837, most of its northern interior was uninhabited and unpenetrated as late as 1900. The building of the first road through the thick forests from Rogers City on Lake Huron into the interior was as herculean a job in the 1880's as had been the building of the National Road in the east in 1822.[66]

This timber country had only been opened by the railroad to Onaway in 1901. One did not have to go west to get the feeling of the pioneer life, and it looked good to Grant. He had a little of the American rolling stone wanderer in his soul anyhow.

Grant and Victorine met later in Detroit, unaware that two births would happen in Michigan in 1909 — their first child and Henry Ford's Model T.,"flivver", or "Tin Lizzie".

They went on board the lake steamer Alpena for the

journey north. The September day was crisp and sunny as the huge paddle wheels pushed the ship into the waters of Lake St. Clair.

The red leather bellows of his Brownie camera were extended for snaps of both of them on the wind swept deck; he in a snappy cap and white vest, very unclerical, and she, slender and smiling, beneath a wide hat with a long shawl for warmth against the lake winds. They were having fun. Victorine, who had never been very far away from home, was enjoying the adventure.

As night came on Lake Huron, there was nothing to see except the black waters and the lights of passing ships. They walked a little on deck, but the dark water made Victorine uneasy.

I remember how black those waters looked in 1918 when my father was moving from Michigan to Ohio. I was eight. When the ship was passing what I now know as Canada, I went out on deck in the night. I asked a man standing at the rail what the lights along the shore were. "Germany", he said roughly. Terrified, I ran back to the safety of our cabin. My head was then full of the "Hun" and the news and propaganda of World War I.

By midnight all was quiet on board The Alpena. The paddles sucking at the water and the walking beam of the engines going up and down were the only things moving. As they approached the lights of Alpena harbor about 2:00 AM, a few sleepy crewmen appeared. On land they went up the long board walk to a little hotel, but only to be up at 5:00 AM for the fifty-mile train ride to Onaway.

The land they saw bore little relation to the scenes they had imagined. A few scraggly farms were cut by homesteaders from the forests on the flat and swampy plains. Then, where logging had been completed, the sea of raw stumps. It was an untidy and exploited land. They arrived exhausted but expectant, only to be told that there was no parsonage to go to because of trouble in the church. Instead, they went to a hotel over one of the town's saloons.

Grant tells the story. "We found there was trouble in the church. A Congregational minister was filling the pulpit. He was very brilliant and had the town coming but he had a drinking problem. He made a hard pull to hold the church, but among the Methodists the Conference rules. He had affected the sale of the parsonage and had leased it for a year. He held out for about a month and then went on a long spree."

Grant felt that the Lord must look down on some of his congregations with disbelief. He wrote: "A banker, treasurer of the church, was wrapped up in the ousted pastor with a note for which the bank's directors were holding him responsible." He was the ousted pastor's principle supporter, insisting to the Bishop that he was the best judge of the local situation. Again, Grant invoked the congregational vote, which he won 146 to 16. After that there was no trouble.

Because he could hunt and fish again as he had in the mountains, Grant enjoyed Onaway. The town stood in the middle of large stands of virgin pines and hardwoods. Its main street had warped wooden sidewalks and coverings of mud when wet and dust when dry. The coming of the Detroit and MacKinac Railroad in 1901 had brought an explosion of lumber-related industries and population. In 1910 it had grown from a village of less than 300 to a lusty 2700. Today it is much quieter at 1400.

Lumber camps ringing the town fueled seven lumber mills, making a variety of products. Economic life was based on lumber as a wasting asset, headlong and careless of the future. Lumbering was done in camps where hundreds of men worked and lived, felling and working the trees out of the forest on wagons of huge wheels, pulled by mules and oxen.

Feeding the lumberjacks was a substantial business. Maybelle Roberts, at ninety, remembers waiting on table in those days for two hundred rough and hungry men, but always under the watchful eye of her Baptist church-going father who ran the camp. One did not have to go west to feel the pulse of a frontier town then.[67]

Class distinctions were unknown because yesterday's lumberjack could today be cutting his own timber. But social life was divided along sharp lines. The lumberjacks supported the seven saloons in the little town, but the church young people organized their own parties and dances, as Grace Prestiger remembers.

Daughter of the town's druggist and doctor, spirited and

independent, Grace had studied dramatics at Grand Rapids to go on the Chautauqua lecture and entertainment circuit, which then played in tents all over America in the summer months. For people then, it was television, radio, the movies, and adult education all rolled into one.

But Grace's father firmly ruled out her traveling with a musical quartet of four men. So early in September, 1909, she married a young banker. A Methodist later, Grace has said that she only joined the Methodist Church (then an enemy of the sins of card playing and dancing) when her dancing days were over.

But she did remember that the minister who conducted her wedding was a little tipsy. For that reason he was not invited to the wedding supper, but he came anyhow. He was the same man who tried to hold onto the church when Grant and Victorine arrived later the same month.[68]

The Masons of Onaway finally made up a purse to send the unfortunate minister to Kansas, the first state of the Union to adopt Prohibition. It was a generous, though probably a useless, gesture. Alcoholism was then seen only as a moral, and not as a medical, problem. There was little understanding of the alcoholic as a sick man, obsessed, living up tight, wanting and hating liquor at the same time, ashamed that he was seen drunk again, vowing that he will never take another drink, but knowing that he will.

Grant's predecessor as minister would sometimes appear at the back door of the drug store of Grace's father to ask for medicinal whiskey for a sick child. The ruse was only a secret to its tragic perpetrator. This experience made Grant hate alcohol all the more.

After the troubled minister had left, the church became more normal. Perhaps my birth on Thanksgiving day 1909, in two cramped rooms where Grant and Victorine had been forced to live at first, had a reconciling influence. Who could long remain angry when the new pastor, his pretty wife, and new baby, were made to live in that way.

25. Grant on the Great Lakes steamer, Alpena, on their way to Onaway, Michigan, September 1909

26. Victorine on the same ship, September 1909

Chapter Twenty-Seven
The Roosevelt-Vatican Incident

In April, 1910, Grant and Victorine were enjoying the new Michigan timber country and their new five-month-old son. That month a minor incident in the world trip of former President Theodore Roosevelt catapulted the Methodist Center at 38 Via Firenze in Rome, where Grant had been four years before, into world-wide publicity.

For some months, Roosevelt had been in Africa. In February, his former Vice President Charles Fairbanks had caused a mild sensation in the American press by refusing to cancel a date to speak at the American Methodist Church in Rome as a condition for being received by Pope Pius X. *The Literary Digest* gave two full pages to the incident. The Catholic *Boston Pilot* made a savage attack on the Methodists at 38 Via Firenze. Some Protestant papers escalated the argument, warning of an impending struggle between The United States and the Roman hierachy.

Fairbanks himself thought the affair trifling and played it down. Just as Fairbanks himself had not been offended, *The Catholic Citizen* of Milwaukee criticized the Vatican diplomats. "These minor incidents stir up people out of all proportion to their real importance. We ourselves will welcome the day when all the diplomats (in the Vatican) will be sentenced to teach catechism to the neglected Italians and sent out of the Vatican." Later all parties would wish that they had exercised some Milwaukee horse sense.[69]

With full knowledge of the Fairbanks incident in February, Roosevelt wrote American Ambassador Leishman in

Rome from Khartoum to arrange an audience with the Italian king and with the Pope. He then received a private message from The Vatican that Pope Pius would be delighted to grant an audience and "he hopes that nothing will arise to prevent it, such as the much regretted incident which made the reception of Mr. Fairbanks impossible."[70]

Ambassador Leishman believed this might be a restriction on Roosevelt's stay and cabled: "One side or the other is sure to make capital out of any action you take."

Although Roosevelt had no plans to address the Methodists anyhow, he did not like being told he could not. Privately, he answered Leishman: "I must decline to submit to any conditions that limit my freedom of action."

John Callan O'Laughlin, an American Catholic who had been assistant Secretary of State for Roosevelt, then tried to straighten out the matter before it broke in the press. He saw Cardinal Merry Del Val, a Spaniard who was Papal Secretary of State. An alert Associated Press reporter got the story of that interview from a Vatican leak.

"Cardinal Merry Del Val said to Mr. O'Laughlin: 'Can you guarantee that Mr. Roosevelt will not visit the Methodists here?' Mr. O'Laughlin said: 'I cannot. He will do as he pleases.'" He then explained that he was not there on Mr. Roosevelt's behalf but for his fellow Catholics in America.

"The Cardinal then said: 'It is not in any sense a question of religion. Mr. Roosevelt might have gone to any church except the Methodist which is carrying on a most offensive program against The Pontiff. The Papal Secretary even recognized Mr. Roosevelt's right to claim the privilege of visiting the Methodists the day after the audience on condition that he, Merry Del Val, had received private assurances that he would not actually do so."

At this time these were private talks and messages. But even before he arrived in Rome, Roosevelt gave out the texts of the private messages to the press. This stunned the Vatican, which had thought, and correctly, that the messages were private and diplomatic. Remembering the Fairbanks hassle, the press was waiting to pounce and did. The matter exploded at once into the atomic mushroom of an international incident.

Reporters fanned out in America to ask religious leaders of all kinds for their comments. The religious press entered the fray. Washington made political humor of the incident, remembering that Roosevelt and his own Vice President had often feuded, saying "for once the President and his Vice President were in the same boat."

"Churchmen were astonished", the *New York Times* said. One young priest refused to give the text of the story handed to him by a reporter to aged Archbishop Farley of New York, because "it would be highly improper to shock him with this news at this hour of the night."

In Catholic but anti-clerical France, the incident was "expected to prove a strong card for the Government in the coming elections in support of M. Briand, the Premier." Some years before, the refusal of the Pope to see President Loubet of France because he had seen the King of Italy first, had led to cutting diplomatic relations between France and the Vatican.

On April 10, the *New York Times* made the Methodist Center at Rome the subject of its entire magazine section. The furor churned on for about two months and then died as quickly as it had begun. Beneath the headlines there were probably hidden motives for the bizarre incident. The *California Christian Advocate* suggested that Cardinal Merry Del Val, a Spaniard, may have resented the humiliation of Spain in the 1898 war. Who better personified that war than the commander of the Rough Riders?

And Teddy himself was not beyond some political suspicion. He had seen the mild sensation created when his former vice president had been refused an audience with the Pope on the same grounds. As he sat in his hot hotel room in Khartoum, he must have thought what would happen if a former American president refused, or was refused, a Papal audience for the same reasons.

The election of 1912, when Roosevelt was to run as a Progressive or "Bull Moose" candidate, after being denied the Republican nomination, was only two years away. At only fifty-two, Roosevelt was vigorous, restless, and disappointed with his successor, William Howard Taft.

Roosevelt must have known what would happen and

thoroughly enjoyed the furor. After he had sent his official version to the magazine, *The Outlook* he had only to assume a dignified silence. Lyman Abbott, the editor, must have been ecstatic to have received such a scoop. Roosevelt was always a political man, and now all America was again reminded of their former Chief.

In the little Methodist Church in Onaway, Grant told the inside story of the events I have just described, as one who had once been at the same church in Rome. He wrote again for *The Methodist Review*.[71]

He reviewed the historic causes of the conflict between the Church and the Italian State. In 1870, Italy had been unified by Garibaldi, and under a new King had granted religious freedom to all. The Methodists at once took advantage of the opportunity.

But the loss of its state went down hard with the Vatican, and the new King was called the "robber" king by the Pope. The Methodist Church at 38 Via Firenze had two churches, the American and the Italian. Fairbanks was to speak to the former, where Grant, as its pastor for a year, had never heard any derogatory word spoken of the Pope.

The bad feeling between the Vatican and the new Italian monarchy led to other bizarre actions. No one could be received by the Pope if he had been received by the Italian King first. To do so "would suggest that the Pope recogized the King".

And then, as one cavalry officer about another, Grant wrote: "And so it is just as well that the ex-President bucked at the first fence, for he would not have submitted to the curb for very long."

Some events that flash spectacularly across our skies are unimportant in themselves but do illuminate how we were. The Roosevelt-Vatican incident of 1910 is one of that kind. It also shows us that the newspapers of 1910 were just as likely to escalate an unimportant event so that it looked important, as television often does today.

Chapter Twenty-Eight
Other Than Theology

This is a story of a time and of a man. As they must always be, the two stories are woven together because each affects the other. Even though religious and classical studies were the main part of his academic work, Grant was also fascinated by the exploding technology and invention of his times. There were things in his life other than theology.

The late nineteenth century and early twentieth century years were a mixture of the bright and hopeful and of an ugly, but incipient, class war. The trauma of the Civil War had faded somewhat. Poverty and discrimination, the legacy of slavery and war, were visited most severely only on one region — the South. The rest of the nation could afford to, and did until much later, ignore the festering sore.

In spite of financial panics, when hard cash (because of the total absence of a central banking system) would disappear like a desert river sucked up in dry sand, the underlying motion of the nation was always forward and the mood fitfully euphoric. Invention and a philosophy of easy and automatic progress were the easy answers to all our problems. With young wonder and astonishment we watched the budding development of electricity, the automobile, and the flying machine.

Before 1916, Grant was a very early and proud owner of a Model T Ford touring car with a bright brass radiator, surely an extravagance for him even at $400. But don't be fooled by the low price. He paid as much in proportion to his income as one would pay for a Ford in 1982. [72]

The Michigan towns we lived in were small and could be

walked with ease. So the excuse that he needed the car for his work was a poor one. Since roads between towns were often impassable in spring and winter, only the bravest tried them in a car. Anyhow, the railroad took you there more quickly and comfortably.[73]

Whatever loving or derisive name you gave it — Model T, Tin Lizzie, Flivver — between 1909 and 1927, the Ford put the whole nation on wheels. An awkward, seven foot tall adolescent, it was nevertheless an advanced car for its day. A 2.9 litre monoblock 4-cylinder engine got twenty five to thirty miles a gallon, and, if pushed, could rattle up to forty miles per hour. It smelled of leather and oil. A bulb horn was squeezed to announce its presence, although that was probably unnecessary because its clanking and rattling had already done so.

Grant didn't drive his Model T. He overcame it, tamed it. He had to learn its moods and when it was going to kick or quit. Starting a Model T Ford was pure art form. First, he advanced the gas control on the steering wheel, carefully, so as not to starve or choke it on ignition. Then he went around to the front and prepared to work the wire circle that served as a choke. He then took hold of the swinging crank, gingerly because of the old wive's tale that it would break your arm if it recoiled.

A vigorous crank. If you were lucky it sputtered to life. He then raced around to the steering wheel to give it more gas. Only the most nimble made it the first time. He sometimes gave me the exacting job of "gassing" it. I would sit tensely behind the wheel with my hand on the gas lever. The trick was to advance it at the exact moment, but not too far.

The transmission was a planetary, two speeds forward and one backwards, activated by three floor foot pedals which had to be worked in proper sequence. The Model T almost never made a smooth start. It jumped forward like a scared rabbit. I would hang tightly on to the sides, while my father would get the beast into some kind of consistent forward motion.

A black canister on the running board held the fuel for the carbide head lamps. In Michigan, we were returning one dark night from a visit in another town. Rain splashed through the cracks in the side curtains. The head lamps revealed about ten feet of the road ahead. At a crossroad my father was uncertain of the way home. A dim kerosene lamp in a farm house nearby told us that we were not the only people left in the world. He asked the way home. He came back to the car cheerfully: "It's down this way eight miles." Eight miles! It sounded like a thousand to me and an eternity until we reached the haven of home.

During the Twenties young men flying "Jennies", World War I trainers, would sometimes land in pastures close to town, promising an air show and rides. Grant would sometimes go out to see them. I had supposed this was only idle curiosity, until I found among his papers at his death an article, apparently never published, *The Conquest Of The Air,* dated 1913.

By 1913, even though only ten years after Kitty Hawk, aviation was leaping forward. Glen Curtis had flown from Albany to New York City. C. P. Rodgers had made it from St. Louis to New York, jumping from pasture to pasture. George Chaves, a Frenchman, had flown over the Alpine passes. In altitude, Hoxey had soared over 11,000 feet in America and Farro over 16,000 feet in France. These were all well researched facts in the article.

But he had also digested the science of flight. He wrote: "They (the Wrights) discovered that the air gave the strongest support to the entering edge of the plane (wing). Hence, the wings were made longer and less deep. They figured out the aspect ratio. That is, if the plane has a spread of 30 feet and a depth of 6 feet, the aspect ratio is 6."

He knew other aerodynamic facts. "The plane (wing) is arched upward from the entering edge to a distance of about one third back, and then slopes to the rear edge. The curve is called the chamber. The plane is driven through the air with the front higher than the rear. This is called the angle of incidence and gives the air a chance to get under and lift." Balance was finally achieved "by arranging flexible tips on the ends of the wings."

I must remember that in 1913 these aerodynamic facts were not yet household words. Men still looked with exciting wonder that men could get off the ground at all.

Finally, he saw more than a flying oddity. "Just what the future is no prophet will dare say. Designers are trying to make the flying machine safer, stronger, and more reliable. The land spaces have been covered, and several daring flyers are now planning to cross the Atlantic. They see a time when regular airplane routes will be established, stations built, tickets sold, and a general traveling public traveling in this way instead of by rail." What a 1913 pipe dream!

Chapter Twenty-Nine

Five Dollars a Day

Their years in Michigan were pleasant for Grant and Victorine. There was plenty of fishing in the spring and hunting in the fall. The salary, though never large, ($1200 a year and house) was sufficient, and they leaned toward a very simple life. This was acceptable because it gave Grant plenty of time for reading and study and removed the necessity of making extra money for extra expenses.

From 1909 until 1915, Grant and Victorine, now with two small boys, Paul and Jack, lived in small Michigan towns, and ministered to small Methodist congregations, Onaway, Vassar, and Lake Orion, the last a lake resort town near Detroit.

While at Lake Orion a famous event in American industrial history on January 14, 1914, prompted Grant to write again for *The Methodist Review,* a happy article that God's hand was finally being seen in industrial and business America. The article showed how intensely interested he was in the public issues of his day.[74]

What was the backdrop scene highlighting this event? At this time America was full of hope, but also of dissension and anger. The inflation of the Civil War was followed by years of deflation. Most people had less and less money for their needs and to pay their debts. And now they could no longer just pick up and get free land.

As Mark Sullivan once said: "The greatest single cause of the mood of irritation and unrest in America in 1900 was the end of free land." Also, ". . . the increase in population out of proportion to the increase in gold (or money), the oppressive practices of the railroads, the rise of trusts and monopolies, the growth of factory life, and the power of organized wealth in politics."[75]

People felt they had no power over their own lives. (In many ways, the same mood prevails in the 1980's, even though the objects of the people's resentment are quite different.)

In the *Methodist Review* Grant wrote: "In the City of Detroit on January 5th, two men, heads of the largest manufacturing concern in the world, sat quietly talking. They were planning to distribute ten million dollars to the employees of their company. These two men were Henry Ford, President, and James Couzens, Secretary, of the Ford Motor Company. The plan involves social democracy in its most concrete form."

Hours were to be reduced to eight a day and the minimum wage was to be five dollars a day. The Ford announcement was a national sensation and resulted in both public praise and private grumbling from Ford's fellow industrialists. But it was in keeping with Ford's maverick character. Three years before, he had won the Seldon patent suit brought against him by the association of Licensed Automobile Manufacturers, an event that freed the entire auto industry from monopolistic control through patents.

Grant wrote exultantly: "God is still a factor in the world and keeps watch over has own. Sobriety, industry, and thrift are to be taught through a sociological department to be established in the main building in the factory. The laborer must establish the fact that he does not spend his money on riotous living. He must also have a disposition to save and prove the same by the addition of money to a savings account." These paternalistic strings were almost certainly to be laughed out of the shop.

The article clearly showed that he shared the general unrest of the times and strongly believed then in Christian social justice. He wrote: "For a long time there has been a deep feeling in the real heart of America, the heart of the square deal and fair play, that things were not going right in industrial America. Labor unrest and large dividends, great wealth and pitiful poverty, are proofs of this."

"Contrary to Divine command, men laid up treasures on

earth. If they did not put their trust in riches, they put their riches in trusts." The trusts were then the conglomerate corporations of his day.

He continued: "The head of a factory often spends hundreds of thousands of dollars on travels abroad and a private yacht, while the men who make his money often live without common comforts. The allotments of life are largely accidental. No man has the right to pride himself on winning great wealth, when in the truest sense he did not earn it."

And The Methodist Church was responding. "Conferences are establishing Commissions on Social Service. The report of that Commission in Detroit in 1913 was an epoch in that body."

In speaking of a man who increased his holdings fifty-one million dollars in six months, the report had said, "No one thinks this man earned this money. The conditions of our industrial life simply made it possible for him to seize it. No Christian has the moral right to be very rich while millions of his brothers are poor."

In the same article, Grant also reported what happened a few days after the famous announcement, and unconciously revealed how desperate the American factory worker really was in 1914.

"The day after the announcement, ten thousand men surged before the factory at Highland Park. The next day twelve thousand. Ford announced that they would take no more men, but the pressure got so great that hoses had to be turned on to disperse the men."

Before we lose ourselves completely in foolish nostalgia for the good old days, think of the meaning of this pitiful scene. Five dollars a day was such a hopeful announcement that thousands nearly rioted. One wonders about the actual condition of workers to whom $1500 a year seemed like riches. For many, the sudden hope froze in their lives as the water from the riot hoses froze on their bodies in the bitter cold of January.

Chapter Thirty

Death And A Memory

Death, unanticipated and cruel, tore Grant and Victorine's happiness into shreds in January, 1915. All my life I have had a haunting memory of a mother who died when I was five. I have touched her living past only once, when in 1967 Blossom, my late wife, and I visited the small Methodist parsonage where we lived when she died at Lake Orion, Michigan. At the time of our visit, it was occupied by the sexton.

It was as I remembered. The parlor, the bedroom on the left with the big double doors where she had lain sick, and my father's study. The only thing missing was the big heating stove in the parlor with its ornamental iron work and isinglass windows. The years telescoped together, and I felt that I had been in that parlor only yesterday. It was a strangely emotional moment.

In the bright autumn of 1973, I wanted to see my mother's grave in Cave Hill Cemetery, Louisville, Kentucky. But first we went to Athens, Ohio, to see our son Edwin and new daughter-in-law, Amy. Then we drove along the banks of the Ohio River on a road called scenic. We crossed at Maysville, Kentucky, a southern-looking town sitting precariously on river bluffs, full of white houses and leaning streets.

In Louisville, I found the place, an older but beautiful cemetery. After the death of my mother in 1915, my brother Jack and I had lived for a while at the McDaniel home in Louisville. So I had been at this spot then. I remembered the open sky, a hill, a green mound of earth, and my father telling me my mother was there. The hill was not as steep as I remembered and a large tree had grown, covering the grave site.

I looked at the simple stone — Victorine McDaniel Perkins, 1887-1915. She had only been twenty-eight on that cold January day when she died in a Detroit hospital. I don't know the real cause of her death, for the death certificate only describes a symptom, clearly showing ignorance of the cause.

I have only a few memories of her. The clearest is the affair of the new toy. My father had brought it to us after an out-of-town trip. It was bright, new, and coveted. My brother Jack and I had been fighting over it, each wanting more than anything else to possess that toy. She leaned down and whispered to me that if I would let Jack have it, I could stay up late that night and play with it.

At once, I was full of generosity toward my little brother. That night remains in my memory with the clarity of a photograph. The soft light of the oil lamp — I was on the floor with the toy, and she was in her rocking chair with her mending. Her face and smile in that soft light are like an old-fashioned sepia snapshot.

But my clearest memory is not of the toy. I don't even remember what it was. It is of the special understanding between us, binding us without words. How could that be? I was not more than four. Do I now feel as an adult what I never felt as a child? I think not. The scene that night has never faded from my memory.

Then there was my first introduction to the music of the piano, a Chickering upright in dark mahogany. Of course, I pounded on it to hear the noise. But once she sat down with me and firmly explained that if I would press every other key, I could make music and not noise. She spread my small fingers and showed me how to do it. I tried it and liked it. I had discovered music and went up and down the keyboard, each new chord a new world. But it was not the piano that eventually claimed me, but the violin, not classical music but square dance orchestras, even now.

Toward the end of my mother's life when she was sick at home, I remember that I was allowed to get into bed with her. I could feel her warmth and see her smile, now touched with suffering. When our four children, Paul, Vickey, little Blossom, and Ed, were very small, we would often wake up in the morning and find one or more of them tucked between us, warm and secure. Remembering my mother, I always knew what a good feeling for a child that was.

Finally, I remember the funeral at the parsonage at Lake Orion and the tears running down my father's cheeks, as he held tightly to me and my brother Jack at the side of the coffin, just before it closed forever on the beautiful one within.

She was so silent. Uncomprehending, I wondered why she did not talk to me. I reached out and touched her.

In the bright fall day fifty-eight years later, remembering, I reached out and touched the stone. My wife, Blossom, stood off to one side, and we did not talk. She was so understanding and knew when to leave me with my thoughts and when to arouse me from them. Blossom has since gone from me and life.

My feelings tumbled around inside me, part bright and part dark. I hardly knew whether I had come here to say goodbye or hello. Victorine's life had paused at twenty-eight. In Heaven she would be expecting her three and five year old boys to run to grasp her fragrant skirt. Seeing gray-haired figures before her would be too much of a shock, and so I am sure that Heaven would not allow such an awkward confrontation.

After Grant's death in 1936, I gathered up his sermons, papers, diaries, letters, and notes, and took them home with me. The years passed, busy and smiling. Night law school, children, career, and community, all the concerns of the immediate present, claimed most of my time and efforts. Every once in a while, I looked into this box of the past. Once I found a poem about his grief at Victorine's death.

"How can we give thee up?
How let the cold grave which opens to receive
Claim from our arms your sacred dust?
That lifelike look of peace still lingers
While yet upon my ears that voice
Whose every accent breathed of tenderness
Is sounding still.

> *Why feel that life for me will still go on*
> *Uncheered by you?*
> *That never again your tender heart*
> *Which shared my every sorrow*
> *Will answer to my own in joy or grief.*
> *That never again your word of counsel or love*
> *As comrade, sister, friend will greet me."*

Taking all the evidence together, her death was unexpected, undiagnosed, and bitterly resented. I once found a scrap of paper in the form of a scribbled note written by Grant to the hospital where she died, but never sent actually in the mails.

"My dear wife has returned from your hospital cured. I would like to do you the honor, provided males are allowed, to present myself at your (an unintelligible word) this afternoon. But I will try not to repay you. Vengeance belongs to God."

Reading this crumpled note, one could feel the depths of his despair and grief.

27. *Victorine's last picture, September 1914, before her death, with her two boys, Paul, on the left, and Jack.*

Chapter Thirty-One

Life Goes On

For Grant's two boys, Paul and Jack, most of the year 1915 was an interlude in the red brick Victorian home of grandfather John McDaniel in Louisville, Kentucky, a time now only dimly remembered.

Remembered. A big black box and a tripod in a strange official-looking place. Grandfather McDaniel was the photographer for the Louisville police department. Remembered. Victorine's two sisters Dedie and Martha and her younger brother Fritz. He laughed a lot and carved boats marvelously out of square blocks of wood.

Remembered. A children's birthday party on a big lawn near a very large and pretentious house, complete with a real merry-go-round. The boys were scrubbed clean, dressed in starched white cotton suits, set down on clean newspapers on the front stoop, and sternly told by their grandmother to stay there until time to go.

Remembered. Visits by their father Grant and, finally, the news that they had a new mother.

The winter of 1915 was as cold as death, lonely and unhappy for Grant at Lake Orion. The parsonage, now empty, was still painfully full of poignant memories — her favorite teapot, a forgotten article of her clothing bringing tears and a deep feeling of sadness, recipes in her hand, her piano no longer filling the house with cascading notes. Only a house now, filled with black loneliness and perhaps anger at her undiagnosed death.

Grant knew he could not stay at Lake Orion another year. His grief was too painful. And, because a minister in those days could not really function without a family, he knew he had to re-establish his. At some Methodist meeting he met Lyla Maxfield, the daughter of an Irish grocer at Brutus, Michigan. She was both a pianist and a singer. He was always drawn toward women with musical talent, perhaps to compensate for his lack of it.

When they married in September 1915, she was twenty-one and he forty-two. Lyla must have, for a moment, hesitated to take on a full family and the demanding job of a minister's wife at the same time. But not for long, for she always had an aplomb at whatever she did.

After their marriage, Grant was assigned to the Methodist Church at Houghton, Michigan, on the wild and timbered upper peninsula of Michigan. Houghton was then the center of copper mining. The open pits of the worked-out mines were everywhere, awesome moonscapes to small boys, who sometimes crept to look over their dangerous edges. Granite was everywhere. In the red stone in the church and other substantial buildings in town. In granite boulders cropping out of the lawns. There was a huge one on one side of the parsonage, a mountain for boys to climb. It is still there, although sunk a little more into the earth.

Located at the base of the big spur that thrusts out into Lake Superior, Houghton was reached then by a railroad that snaked through the forests or by a ship canal that carried the ore boats to the east. The street dropped steeply to the canal, so much so that a Model T Ford could only get up the hill if it had a full tank of gas. Of course, it could always back up because the gasoline was gravity-fed forward to the motor.

The streets were tough on cars in the winter, but what a sled run! Sleds had the streets to themselves. Automobiles wintered in garages.

The Daily Mining Gazette, published every day in what was really a small town, reveals what an important industrial center Houghton was. There were extensive daily stock and commodity reports in its columns. The editor interviewed the new minister on Sunday, September 26, 1915. Grant was described as a "southern abolitionist" in family, and a Spanish War captain. The reporter concluded: "He is a big upstanding man, of athletic appearance and a good sense of humor."

The title of his first sermon at Houghton, "A Christian's Marching Orders", unconsciously uncovered our slowly growing awareness of an ugly war in Europe moving our way. In a year and a half America would be swept into it. On July 4, 1916, a daughter Gwen was born to Grant and Lyla. But the firecrackers bursting all over town were not really for her. Confined to their room his sons were not allowed out until the mid-wife showed them a new baby sister.

True to its itinerant tradition, the Methodists sent Grant to Gladstone, Michigan, in September, 1916. It was on a bay on the west side of Lake Michigan, near Wisconsin. There, Grant introduced his eldest son, at age eight, to fishing, a sport the son never pursued again. As a lakeport, Gladstone shipped a lot of new timber on lake schooners combining sail and steam. The schooners, their decks piled high with lumber, made a colorful sight.

The debris from the lumber mills would drift against the shore. To fish in deeper waters, one only had to crawl gingerly out a few feet on this thick and undulating mass, drop in bamboo poles, and take out as many perch as wanted. Grant never knew his boys sometimes tried the risky business without him.

At Gladstone, there were chickens in the back yard and a war garden behind the church next door. Chicken thieves kept depleting the flock. Grant arranged a line and a bell to give a signal in the house, if the chicken house door was opened during the night. One night the bell rang. Through the back room to the roof over the back porch came Grant, bathrobe flying, sans his toupee, shotgun ready. He found the chickens agitated; but the thief, whether man, boy, racoon, or fox, had vanished.

Remembered also, a moment of terror at Gladstone. Near town, there was a pine woods that caught fire one day. Looking for the fire, Grant's boys went into the woods. The smoke, at first rather light, began to thicken. Suddenly Paul lost his little brother in the pall. He was scared, but more terrified because he could not find his brother. In a few moments Jack re-appeared, and Paul has never been so glad to see anyone since. They got out of there in a hurry.

At Gladstone, Grant's boys were allowed to watch the dark and mysterious process of developing pictures. A camera buff, Grant had followed that hobby since 1904. His No. 3 Folding Brownie Camera still takes good sharp pictures. The kitchen was darkened, solutions prepared in pans, and a dark red light turned on. One watched, big-eyed, as the little square of white paper began to form the human shape. And there Paul was flying his kite.

Grant even tried flash light pictures at night. A notable one was a Christmas tree: its toys ranged beneath with the wind up train, the circus animals of carved wood, and the red metal fire engine. Powder was distributed in a pan held high above his head. There was no automatic flash. One had to click the camera and explode the powder at the right time. Hands were to ears as all waited in awful suspense. The flash came and the acrid smoke rolled out into the room. Taking pictures was a real adventure then.

His boys first became aware of Grant as a minister at Gladstone. When in the pulpit, with his black formal coat with tails, and striped trousers, they dimly understood there was another dimension to their father. In the church service, his first act was always the same. He knelt at his chair in private prayer, and then rose to conduct the service. It was always a hushed moment.

28. Grant and Lyla, September 1915

29. Grant and his 1916 Model T in Michigan

Chapter Thirty-two
Public Issues of 1917

Grant was intensely interested in the important and passionate public issues of his day. He was not isolated in his religion. Today, there is a contradiction in American life. Even as technology has been perfected and instant and voluminous communication has grown by leaps and bounds, the interest of most Americans in public affairs has plummetted. This was not true in 1917.

When Grant was in Gladstone, Michigan, in 1917, two important public issues reached a climax — the European war (not yet called World War I) and the national prohibition of alcoholic drink.

Easily the most exciting event for Grant was the runaway victory of prohibition in several state elections in November, 1916. With Woodrow Wilson's close re-election on the slogan "He kept Us Out Of War", that conflict did not seem near. Yet war came with stunning speed on April 6, 1917; and the prohibition amendment passed in Congress in November, 1917, in an aura of sacrificial emotion, and was submitted to the states for ratification.

Sentiment for prohibition had been growing for many years. Beginning in Maine in 1846, states had been voting on state prohibition for a long time. But Americans were ambivalent. How they blew both hot and cold is revealed in the State of Massachusetts which voted dry in 1852, wet in 1868, dry in 1869, and wet again in 1875.

It is hard now to recreate the emotions and controversies generated by prohibition. But for Grant, abstinence was not only an article of faith of the Methodist Church (now relaxed a little) but also a matter of personal conviction. He had seen so much drunkenness in the mountains and in the army that there was no middle ground for him.

Prohibition was deeply divisive and totally failed to reach its objective, despite its good intentions. It failed because it ignored those natural limits to law which Supreme Court Justice Holmes once described: "The first requirement of a sound body of law is that it should correspond with the actual feelings and demands of the community, whether right or wrong."[76]

While the conflict raged during tha last half of the nineteenth century, both sides used demagogic arguments. The wets called beer liquid bread and liquor a nutrituous food. The drys claimed that those who drink have children with weak minds. It is generally true that the whole history of dry and wet medical propaganda was a history of misrepresentation.

As early as 1905 Grant had written about the controversy that raged when Congress had abolished the post canteens at army forts. He wrote then: "While Congress had only intended to abolish that part of the canteen that sold liquor, the army with its usual method of interpreting the law, abolished the whole canteen."

But still he approved: "I have seen service where there was no post saloon and one where one was running full blast. In the first, a class of men would leave the post on being paid, get drunk, and remain so until lack of money drove them back to their summary court martials. Disorder in the garrison was unusual. But at the post saloon revelry reigned supreme. All drills were suspended for two or three days after the paymaster's visit."

In American history, drunkenness once contributed to an important American military victory. If the Hessians had not been drinking at Trenton, New Jersey, Washington might not have had his victory there at a low point in the Revolutionary War.

Grant's opinion on the army canteen was not the majority opinion in the army. Army officer wife, Martha Summerhayes, once wrote bitterly: "Those estimable women of the W C.T.U. (Women's Christian Temperance Union) thought to do good for the army no doubt, but through their pitiful ignorance of the soldier's need have done him incalculable harm. The canteen provided them with a place where they could go, read, chat, smoke, or play some games, and escape the lonesomeness of the barracks."[77]

Prohibition was the first attempt to regulate the private and non-violent behavior of people by a national law. The volatile and constitutionally dangerous ingredients are always the same — a public issue with strong religious and emotional overtones and a well-organized and financed and militant political action group. The danger to America is always that, with such a combination, we sometimes take leave of our usual constitutional good sense. The passions of temporary majorities on narrow specific subjects should never be made a part of the Constitution, no matter how desirable they seem at the moment.

In the case of Prohibition, the political action group was the Anti-Saloon League, founded at Oberlin, Ohio, in 1893. It organized the fragmented Protestant churches into a powerful and effective lobby. It concentrated on legislation as well as public relations and education. It worked up through hundreds of local, county, and state elections to national prohibition. It was savage with any elected official or representative who differed from its bone dry views. And it had the advantage of an ultimate and simple objective — national prohibition by constitutional amendment. It became the most important dry organization. Most of the credit for bringing on prohibition must go to this militant body.

This was the background which prompted Grant to write again for the *Methodist Review.* Michigan had voted dry and he was exultant and felt this almost assured a constitutional amendment by 1920. He had a clear understanding of the political ramifications of prohibition. "Out in Indiana, a wet senator and ten wet congressmen were retired. Up in Michigan one Mr. Beaks placed his political fortune with the wets. Another now sits in his place."[78]

He clearly understood the constitutional limitations of the federal government. Without a constitutional amendment, the Congress could only act to control liquor traffic if it was in interstate commerce. He wrote that "Congress ought to exclude booze advertisements from the mail, stop interstate shipments of liquor, and withhold federal licenses in dry states."

In 1916 twenty-five states had voted dry, or nearly dry. With thirty-six states needed to ratify any prohibition amendment, he felt that it was as sure as mathematics. But he was also troubled by the loss of property and investment. "There is one phase of the question that gives thoughtful men concern, the seeming destruction of property." But there were other uses for these properties. "Henry Ford has suggested Michigan brewers make wood alcohol, and Henry is thought to have worked out a practical method of making it the coming fuel for his automobiles."

Grant closed the article by setting a time limit, "namely to write prohibition into the fundamental law of the land and so fence and guard it that never again will alcoholic beverages prey upon the life blood of the nation, and to do this by 1920". He was right on the mark. The Eighteenth Amendment became law, January 16, 1920.

The nineteen twenties brought Prohibition's debacle, the gangster, and an America which continued to vote for prohibition and to go to the speakeasy at the same time. The repeal of Prohibition in 1933 was a bitter disappointment to Grant. Although he had once voted for Woodrow Wilson as President, such Republican apostasy vanished in his fierce defense of the "noble experiment", as Herbert Hoover called Prohibition in 1928.

And so, in the election of 1932, Grant and his oldest son parted political company. That summer I and three other unemployed college graduates started a weekly newspaper in Alliance, Ohio. It was a shoe-string operation in which we sold enough ads to pay the printing bill, to distribute it by hand, and to make a little for ourselves. There were strong editorials for Franklin Roosevelt in the short-lived *Alliance Chronicle.* But Grant never forgave the Democrats for bringing back the booze, even though it had never really gone away.

Chapter Thirty-three
YMCA Hut At Camp Sherman

By the end of 1916 the European War had already drawn millions of English, French, Germans, Russians, Austrians, and Italians into its whirlpool of death and the United States close to its spinning edge, in spite of the campaign slogan in the elections that year. Woodrow Wilson "had kept us out of war." Maybe it was only half believed.

At the start of 1917 the Imperial German government announced, and its submarines began, unrestricted submarine warfare, with the result that it sank the largest tonnage of allied ships in April. Wilson's Secretary of War Lansing favored war partly because he felt that would encourage the democratic elements in Germany and Russia. Even though the Kerensky provisional government in Russia had toppled the Czar in February, it was still in the war and still parliamentarian in the western sense.

President Wilson was hesitant about pushing the country into the unknown pit of war, but his cabinet unanimously advised him to seek a declaration of war from the Congress. That tipped the scales and on April 2, 1917, Wilson asked for a declaration of war. As was its right under a Constitution more clearly understood than it is today, Congress declared war on Germany on April 6th. There were six votes in the Senate and fifty in the House against it.

To some in the country who had not been listening, war came as a surprise, but not to Grant in the little Methodist parsonage at Gladstone, Michigan. He suddenly saw his journal as a student in Leipzig in a new light, because what he had seen and felt in 1905 almost foretold what was happening in 1917.

Because he had seen the Prussian officer at first hand and had heard with what fervor students had sung of "Deutschland Uber Alles", he was not surprised about the war. In the nineteenth century Prussian militarism had impressed its stamp on the other German states; and the armies, strategies, armaments, and military organization of Imperial Germany were in 1914 superior to anything in Europe.[79]

Of course, Grant only saw and perceived what filtered through the censors and the propaganda of the Allies. The awful carnage of the battles of 1916 was almost completely hidden behind the censor's screen. The English public itself hardly knew that several hundred thousand men had fallen in the first battle of the Somme in 1916.

From his little private corner of the world, Grant observed these rapidly accelerating events more and more restlessly. I am sure that he tried to get back into the army, but at forty-four and with a history of malaria, that was impossible.

But the YMCA offered another way to get into at least a part of the war. Forgotten is the important role that organization played in World War I. The YMCA operated in every place where Americans trained or served, and handled nine-tenths of the welfare work among American forces in Europe. "Just before the armistice in 1918, it had 1397 stations in France. During the five years following the war, it gave educational assistance to more than 100,000 ex-servicemen studying at schools and colleges."[80] By autumn of 1917 Grant was at Camp Sherman at Chillicothe, Ohio, as educational Secretary of the Y.

After 1918, he wrote about his experiences in an article called "When the Division Moved." Two divisions were at Camp Sherman, when the order came for the entire 83rd division to move to its secret point of embarkation for France. The YMCA had sixteen centers or huts scattered throughout the camp; and when over 30,000 men were ordered out, this is what happened.

"I had come directly from the Association College in Chicago where the course had been cut short because of the great need for Y workers a few weeks before the 'pack up' order was issued. When this order was read at retreat, the real fun began. The enthusiasm of the men was boundless. They wanted to get over and at the big job before them, and they believed it could not last long after they arrived.

"All of the men wanted to go home for a short furlough, but this was impossible. Being denied that, they wanted their folks at home to come to the camp, and 20,000 men beseiged the telephone and telegraph booths in the huts. At the same time news had gone out that the division was under orders to move, and tens of thousands on the outside tried to get messages to their soldier kin on the inside.

"Very few of the thousands of telephone calls ever got through, and I have known the telephone girls to break down and cry at the sense of their helplessness, when all wanted the line at the same time.

"Service by telegram was better because it could be received and filed and sent later. For a day or so, the Y force was swamped and there was no sleep, but every telegram was sent.

"Field equipment meant the elimination of every gift, trinket, or souvenir the soldier had with him in camp. His pack must weigh only forty-two pounds, and the government had that much equipment to fill it. In camp "Sammy" could have anything he wanted, but overseas it would be different.

"So it came about that 36,000 men had parcel post packages to send home within a few days. The Y was the unofficial post office, and ninety percent of the mail was taken to the Y huts. The Y furnished the wrapping paper, cord, and manpower, weighed and marked the packages. The boys furnished the stamps. These packages, stacked in neat piles, would fill half the social room and reach nearly to the rafters. Mail trains in Chillicothe would be held up two or three hours, in order to take on the parcels from the camp. The secretaries stayed by, beginning at 5:30 AM to well past 11:00 PM

"In this crisis the Y became absolutely essential. The government was not prepared and could not possibly have handled the mail from one central office in so short a time.

"One story was of a mother who had journeyed across the state to see her son but forgot his regiment and company. The Community Center in Chillicothe called Hut 71, and

I accepted the task of helping her. It looked like an impossible task to find the boy among two divisions of 60,000 men, but after many inquiries we located him and brought mother and son together the last Sunday afternoon of the division's stay in Camp Sherman.

"Another boy's wife had come to spend the last Sunday with him, but he was read out for special duty that would prevent her seeing him. He was sitting on the bench outside the hut crying like a baby. I sat down beside him and he told me his trouble. The captain was seen, and his detail was changed so that he could get back at 4:00 PM. He was given a pass for Sunday and Sunday night. From a broken and despondent lad, and his unhappy wife, they parted in high spirits.

"We stood with tear-dimmed eyes as the 83rd marched away, and then our part of the camp was still as death.

"It was the second day after the division had moved that a father, mother, and two sisters came in to see one of our lads now on his way 'over there'. I shall never forget the perfect blank, the disappointment incarnate, and the tears when I told them the regiment had gone. 'Where?' they asked. 'To the port of embarkation' I said. 'But he didn't say that they were to go at once,' they cried. I had to explain that no one knew the day they were to go and that the movements of the trains had to be kept secret.

"Son and brother had gone overseas, and perhaps they would never see him again. They could have come on Sunday but they never thought they would be gone so soon. One who served as a Y man can never forget those days, nor do any of us ever want to see another war to tear asunder the ties of life and love."

It was in September, 1917, that Grant had decided to move his family to Conneaut, Ohio, on the eastern shores of Lake Erie. The minister of the First Methodist Church there was himself in Y work in France, and, by commuting by train to Chillicothe, Grant could preach there on Sunday.

We came to Ohio in a Great Lakes passenger side wheeler. They once filled these incomparable inland seas, calling at every important and unimportant town on their shores. Their huge awkward side wheels churned along at about ten knots. They have vanished in a society which now values speed as the only ultimate good.

But to children in 1918 the voyage was a great adventure. My brother and I had the run of the ship and explored every corner, including some we were not supposed to explore.

30. Grant at Camp Sherman as a Y man, 1918

Chapter Thirty-Four
Antioch College 1919

The end of World War I brought anxious moments to Grant and Lyla. In taking temporary work at Conneaut, Ohio, and with the YMCA, he had to move from the Michigan Conference of the Methodists to the Ohio Conference.

The importance of these Conferences is quite lost on an outsider. Methodist ministers do not belong to a national church, but to one of these Conferences; and their importance is that appointments to churches, programs, and even pensions are decided on the conference level. A minister from outside the Conference must first be accepted only on trial, and could not just walk in as a matter or right. He worried how he would fare as a stranger in Ohio.

But suddenly, later in 1918, a different job opportunity opened up for Grant. Fresh from its wartime successes, the YMCA, with the same ebullience that created 1300 YMCA army huts during the war, planned to get into higher education.

In February, 1919, Grant attended a meeting of the trustees of Antioch College at Yellow Springs, Ohio, with a plan to make it a national YMCA college. H.A. Truesdale, a Conneaut businessman speaking for the Y, was enthusiastic about raising $500,000 in endowment. "Antioch is going to have it," he said.[81]

Antioch had been started by the famous Massachusetts educator Horace Mann in 1853. Born in 1796, a member of the Massachusetts legislature, in religion a Calvinist turned Unitarian, Horace Mann had been intensely interested in practical and humanitarian reforms. Ha had been known for far reaching reforms in public education in Massachusetts, as the first elected Secretary of Education in any state.

In 1919, Antioch was small and distinguished, but at a low point in its history. The war had drained away its young men, and only a few were returning. Its trustees knew that it was touch and go whether it could remain open. So the plan looked good to some of the trustees and particularly to a faculty member W W. Weaver who also spoke for the Y.

All these years, Antioch had firmly stuck by its original liberal non-sectarian and co-educational charter. So one trustee was skeptical and questioned the original conservative evangelical character of the YMCA. Grant, fresh from his war work with the Y, assured him that the Y had served all and had left such narrow restrictions behind. It had in the war served alike Catholics, Jews, Unitarians, Quakers, and Evangelicals, he said. Very diplomatic. He must have known that Horace Mann had been a Unitarian.

The trustees of Antioch approved the YMCA plan in principal, and elected Grant president and member of the Board. He was not to take office until June, and with the further understanding that representatives of the Y would raise $500,000 in endowment.

There were tensions present, even though the vote was unanimous. Grant sensed them. A reluctance to turn over such an old wise college to a brash newcomer. Worry over the retention of old faculty members. Suggestions that they were moving too fast. Some resignations on the board of trustees were tendered to allow YMCA representatives to be elected. But, quietly, Grant suggested at one point that no more resignations be offered. He wanted local members to remain.

With elation he told Lyla that night that the Y plan had been approved. He remembered an earlier chance in 1905 to enter college life had been turned aside. But there was no hesitation now.

Moving to Yellow Springs early in 1919, his family of five occupied the house that Horace Mann had built in 1855. It would go by fire in 1924. It was a monstrosity for Lyla to clean and take care of, but what a place for two small boys and a smaller girl, Gwen.

The kitchen was nineteenth century Victorian. A huge library with an ornate fireplace had space for ten times Grant's considerable library. It was three stories of yellow brick, topped by a large "widows walk" and surrounded on all four sides by a deep open porch.

The porch was a favorite race track of Grant's boys, Paul and Jack. Only a few of the many rooms of the house were needed, and so the entire upper two stories were empty. The modest furniture of a small town Methodist preacher was never intended to fill the mansion of such a famous person. In those upper stories there were dark and echoing rooms and stairways leading both up and down to mysterious caverns in the house. The boys often played in those labyrinthine depths, with the delicious small boy feeling that they may come on a ghost or a skeleton.

It was also the year of the locust, for the sidewalks were thick and crunchy with flying creatures that summer. The boys' introduction to baseball came at Antioch, because the college field was just across the street from their house. The crack of the bats, the thud of the ball, and the excitement of the game were exciting fare for them. Most of the players were in army uniforms, boys just back from World War I.

But the grandiose and hopeful plans of the YMCA faltered. The reaction to the war was already setting in, and the Y found that it was not as easy to raise money as it had been during the war. It was not able to raise five hundred thousand dollars in endowment, and so the plan to buy Antioch was abandoned in May, 1919. Grant resigned as president in that month, and went on to work with the Methodist Centenary at Columbus. Mr. Truesdale's enthusiasm apparently exceeded his reach.

Antioch did not perish. In 1920, Arthur Morgan came and made it into the famous co-operative college where students worked part of the year in industries, often related to their college work, and went to school part of the year. With regret that his new adventure had faded, Grant prepared to go back into the ministry.

31. The Horace Mann Home at Antioch College, about 1890

Chapter Thirty-Five
Normalcy 1920

"Normalcy" as a desirable state of national being was first conceived in the shallow and unformed mind of Warren G. Harding during the election of 1920. But it did fit the mood of Americans, who were weary of the magnificent vistas of war and the unattainable goals of peace. With the loosening of old mores that wars and the end of wars always brings, America was already beginning the "Roaring Twenties".

To Grant and Lyla, "normalcy" in September, 1919, meant another move and the anxious uncertainty of Conference days in the Methodist Church. Because this was their fifth move since 1915, Lyla especially longed for a more permanent home; but the sons, at least, never tired of such a kaleidoscopic life. Each new town was a new adventure, a new house to explore from top to bottom, a new neighborhood to poke around in, new boys their own age toward whom they would hold out suspicious overtures. They were sometimes scorned because they were preacher's kids.

Of course, the new school was often a fearful threshold. Silently and uncomfortably, one would walk beside father as they went through the noisy ragamuffin crowd of staring peers on their way to the principal's office. Although the boys were only being curious, as cattle in a field will gather around a newcomer staring, they often seemed hostile to newcomers.

Getting to the new home was always the greatest adventure of all. Except when they came from Michigan to Ohio by ship on the Great Lakes, it was always by railroad. The children came to love the pungent odor of the steam engine, the green velour of the car seats, the long aisles for running, the curtains closed around the snug harbor of the lower berth, the stinging fly ash of the engine drifting in the open windows, and the terrifying crash and rush of the passing train on the next track. They would still rather go to heaven by train than by jet.

Once in mid-winter, they crossed the Straits of Mackinac between southern and northern Michigan on a train ferry. The engine and all its cars simply crawled into the mammoth open mouth of the ferry, which in their fertile imaginations, at eight and ten, looked like a pre-historic monster. When they were inside, the huge lip closed noisily, shutting them in the ferry's gut. They escaped to the upper deck and watched the powerful bow churn and crunch the ice underneath like paper confetti.

With the withdrawal of the YMCA in May from the Antioch College plan, Grant knew he would have to take an appointment in the Northeast Ohio Conference of the Methodist Church. Because he was new to this Conference, he was anxious about this, because he did not have the rank, seniority, or acceptance he had built up in the Michigan Conference.

Although he was also living through the momentous national events of that year, his worries about his family and career were on the top of his mind. We all have a curious relationship to the public events of our lives. They affect us deeply although only indirectly and seem remote to our daily worries. In 1919 Grant lived in one of the most dramatic and tragic years of our history.

The drama was the League of Nation's debate, and the tragedy was that of President Woodrow Wilson. In January, 1919, Wilson had arrived in France for the opening of the peace conference at the peak of his power and popularity; and to such a tumultuous reception that "the demonstrations actually terrified experienced newspaper reporters".[82] Yet, at the close of 1919, he was broken in health and defeated in his purpose.

In January, he had quietly determined to frame this treaty for peace and not for revenge; and as early as February saw a draft of the League of Nations adopted by the Peace Conference. As a practical conservative, Clemencau of France only believed in peace by force and was amazed that Wilson really meant what he said. Still the League survived in the Treaty; and Wilson brought it back to America, confident in his Calvinist soul that it was of God and for the ages. Of course, it was neither. Since the United States never ratified the Treaty of Versailles, the League was born and died a cripple. "For the ages" meant seventeen years until Hitler occupied the Rhineland in 1936 and rolled on to World War II.

The nationwide speaking tour that Wilson undertook in September, 1919, to save the League came at the same time that Grant was attending the Ohio Methodist Conference; and he read the dramatic headlines in the newspapers: "Denver Thunders Approval and Support for Wilson" or "50,000 Strive to Hear Wilson" (San Francisco).[83] There were many signs that the country was moving to his side. Believing this, Wilson drove himself with such determination that a stroke cut him down in his train September 25, 1919. At the climax of the fight, he was knocked out of it. The practical men took charge. Because Wilson stubbornly refused any compromise, the League died in the Senate November 19, 1919, and the Wilson Presidency faded and died.

I doubt that the men who heard Wilson on September 5, 1919, at the luncheon meeting of the Saint Louis Chamber of Commerce ever really knew that they were staring into the reality of 1939 and World War II. With the desperate, but clear-eyed, prescience of an Old Testament prophet, Wilson told his audience: "You fought for something you did not get. There will come in the vengeful Providence of God another struggle, in which, not a few hundred thousand fine men from America will have to die, but as many millions as are necessary to accomplish the final freedom."[84]

But these national events did not worry Grant as much as his private worries. He once wrote about that Ohio Conference: "I was introduced to a committee from Wesley Church in Massillon. They told me the average stay of a pastor had been two years. A restless group demanded a change, sometimes every year. It was the first and only time in the Methodist Church I ever had a chance to sit down with a local group. I was assured five years or more and was to have the benefit of the increase if I developed the field. (If he was to increase the number of members) I had made my own bed in the Kentucky and Michigan conferences, and I felt I could do it again. The satisfaction in the ministry is the feeling that you live from your own labor and not from another's."

Grant told Lyla it was Massillon. Because she was the one who had to make it stretch, she asked what the salary was. $1300 a year and house, with the promise of an increase. She thought that Methodist ministers might as well take the Catholic vows of poverty because that is what they get anyhow.

And so the boxes and the barrels came out again, and Lyla, an expert in the logistics of packing by now, told us how to stow away our humble and battered household goods. The deer head on the wall simply disappeared during one move, discarded because Lyla said it was impossible to pack. But at Massillon, Lyla had part of her wish come true because Grant had five good years there until 1924; and the church made good its other promise, doubling his salary to a magnificent $2700 a year.

Although Grant did not know it in 1919, the church at Massillon was the high water mark of his professional career. Except for the last church at Willard, Ohio, where he died in 1936, the churches he served after Massillon were all smaller and humbler.

Yet he must have suspected by this time that he was not to become a popular or "successful" preacher. Ernest Perkins, Grant's second cousin and full of 86 years of Kentucky hill wisdom, told us in 1974 that, about 1910, Grant had held some revival meetings in Bear Creek Chapel at Meadowcreek. With what proud hopes Grant must have planned those meetings in the little church where his father had preached in 1870. The meetings did not come off well. Angered at the lack of response of the Meadowcreek folk, Grant had told them that the only difference between hell and Meadowcreek was that the latter had a creek running through it. For this Ernest gave him a mild rebuke.

Very early in his career, it was clear that Grant could influence people better than crowds. His thoughts did not flow in vague emotional streams, but were stamped out of deep thought, not easy to understand. At least I understood and liked that better.

The years at Massillon were stable and satisfying to Grant. But they were touched with the bitter controversy over Prohibition, which was already starting to produce, as it did in the nation, the subculture of organized bootlegging in Massillon, a tough steel town. Grant was in the middle of a fight to remove a police chief for not enforcing prohibition. There was trouble for him in that. One midnight, rocks pelted our house and broke windows. In that time, an opponent invited Grant to fight it out. But the six foot-three minister took off his coat and approached the challenger ready for the fight. His opponent was so shocked at this unexpected behavior of a Methodist minister, he just faded away.

We boys were only faintly aware of such things, and lived the hedonistic life of pre-adolescent American boys in the twenties, inventing our own pre-television entertainment: playing football and baseball on the bare clay school ground of Emerson school; going to (and sometimes sneaking into) the games of a semi-pro baseball team, the Massillon Agathons; taking violin and piano lessons with the greatest reluctance; reading western pulp magazines, often in the crotch between two branches of a maple tree in our yard (the only safe place, because Lyla thought westerns were degrading and would take them away from us); swimming unsupervised in the Tuscarawas River and other waters; and taking a mild interest in a bright chip of a sister, Miriam, born in 1920.

For the first time in his life at Massillon, Grant had a little extra money, maybe not because of his earnings but because of Lyla's frugality. At this time, Grant and Lyla managed to buy one summer cottage and then to build another at Lakeside, Ohio, an old Methodist camp ground and summer meeting place on Lake Erie. They were raw, unfinished, frame affairs, smelling of pine. Here we spent two delightful weeks each summer, getting there in our Model T Ford, a day long trip of one hundred miles.

The Lakeside cottages were also an investment, because they were rented to others for the rest of the summer season. Otherwise, Grant was not a sophisticated investor. When Germany was in the middle of its currency inflation, Grant proposed that he invest in German marks, by this time mere paper fluff. But Lyla had saved him with a firm and wise no.

Chapter Thirty-Six
"Hardscrabble Hellas"

In the autumn of 1923, Grant began a thirteen year struggle to educate his sons and daughters on a salary that never rose above $3000 a year and, during the depression years, sank far below. At Washington High School in Massillon, Ohio, my first two weeks as a freshman were normal enough; but then I was shipped off to Sue Bennett School, a little private Methodist Academy in London, Kentucky.

Although I recall little about grade school, I clearly remember at Washington High my surprise and intellectual pleasure in solving the first problems in that esoteric science, algebra. At London, Kentucky, I was met at the train by a Perkins cousin, a tall cheerful Kentucky mountain boy with whom I roomed in the boy's dormitory at Sue Bennett, a simple building with only a coal grate in each room for warmth in winter. That was normal for Kentucky then.

But Grant wanted more personal control over me closer to home. Sometime in the summer of 1924, he drove our archaic second-hand Chevrolet to Western Reserve Academy at Hudson, Ohio, to see to other arrangements for the education of his sons. Only by looking back, do I now realize how quietly, but fiercely determined, he was. The fight he made for the education of his children was simply an extension of his own fight to escape the poverty of the mountains. Even though he had only exchanged that for the poverty of the ministry, he knew at least that he was no longer poor in spirit, the most degrading poverty of all.

Believing that all good things were possible through education, Grant still lived in that age of innocence. What was

Western Reserve Academy? In Hudson, Ohio, south of Cleveland about twenty-five miles, there was a campus of old red brick Georgian buildings, looking like New England in the days of Emerson. This part of Ohio had been the Western Reserve of Connecticut before the American Revolution. New England pioneers had brought their architecture and customs with them, and also their zeal for education. Founded as Western Reserve College in 1826, with the academy as a department, the college had been lured by industrial wealth to move to Cleveland in 1882, leaving the Hudson campus to the Academy. The Cleveland institution is now Case-Western Reserve University.

The Academy had struggled to stay alive, but had died in 1901, its magnificent old buildings decaying on a weed-grown campus. This was a sad sight to James W. Ellsworth who had returned to his boyhood home at Hudson from a successful business career in Chicago, to build a country estate, Evamere Hall, on a farm near Hudson. He had attended the academy in the 1860's. He made it a work of the rest of his life to rebuild, restore, re-open, and hover over every detail of Western Reserve Academy, which had re-opened in 1916.

When James Ellsworth died in 1926, he willed over four million dollars to little Reserve Academy. In February, 1927, author Lucien Price, who had been a student during the hard days of 1901, wrote a delightful piece in the Atlantic Monthly, titled " Hardscrabble Hellas."

> "There is a lost fatherland for which the modern world goes homesick. Yet not always lost, for at odd times, in obscure places, it lives again. And this was the distinction (for the high gods delight to visit the humble) which befell a poverty-stricken academy in a Middle-Western small town. Queerly disguised this ancient fatherland was, but exiles know home when they see it . . . Such was the passion which this out-at-elbow transplantation of Periclean Athens enkindled in a handful of young barbarians at play. It was the miracle which the whole world of education goes seeking . . . So I tell the story of this harrassed school as it was a quarter of a century ago, a story with an end-

> *ing which, had it been predicted to us then, would have sounded like the most extravagant of poets' dreams . . . Poor dear little old Hardscrabble. So now you are rich. We have seen what the school could do without money. Now what can be done with it."*[85]

As Grant walked under the nave of the elms of a campus still ragged from its years of neglect, he wondered anxiously about his reception. He knew he could not possibly afford to send my brother and me there without substantial help. The new young headmaster, Ralph Boothby, came out of his office in Seymour Hall to greet his tall, but slightly stooped, visitor. Boothby had just come to Reserve a few months before and had already decided tht he wanted to create there "an aristocracy of character rather than of wealth".

As they talked together, they happily discovered that they had both been at Harvard, Columbia, and Antioch. Boothby, a Harvard graduate of 1912, had been in the graduate school of Columbia, and, after teaching at private schools, in 1922 had been a professor of education at Antioch.

Mr. Ellsworth had given Boothby a scholarship fund, but the scholarship that he offered Grant's two sons for the autumn class of 1923 was not because of their modest but adequate I.Q.'s. Very likely the real reason was these two quiet philosophers just took a liking to each other. To me, it was just a lucky fall of the cards that they met at that time and place.

Even though the yearly cost at the Academy was only $600 and there was a scholarship and a part time job, the drain on Grant's meager salary must have been severe.

But the best in education was what the Academy had been in 1923, and still is. Lucien Price writing about it in 1927 as it was in 1901, said:

> *"I have dwelt on the poverty and meagerness of this school in order that no-one might suppose that we are discussing education de-luxe. The current idea is that you must have gilt-edged equipment. But that forlorn school had the one thing needful — delight in hard mental exercise. Delight in sharp physical exercise*

boys know in their games. Instinct sees to that. Yet this other delight is well within the grasp of boyhood, and lucky is the boy who grasps it early, for it arms him with one of the few weapons which may enable him to cope with other instincts more unruly."[86]

At the Academy between 1924 and 1927, the Roaring Twenties may have been all around; but in this disciplined, but loosely governed, retreat, its boys were only dimly aware of it. For all its libertine reputation, the twenties were an innocent time for them.

They were absorbed in school life. There was a place on a team for all, even the left-footed; daily music and chapel; lights out at ten; the close camaraderie of one hundred thirty boys; a naturally stern but non-authoritarian daily touch of our teachers. Those who took French sat at a French table in the dining hall and tried to speak no English. In senior history Mr. Mickel followed the arms limitation talks of 1927 and they debated whether the Nation should scrap any of its magnificent battleships. They would become the extinct dinosaurs of the Navy anyhow, so temporary is the massive present.

One day a week was spent at Evamere farm, although the resident farmer must have wished that they would get out of his way. The boys wrote and edited their own newspaper, *The Record,* with guidance, but little interference, from a faculty advisor. A class artist and sculptor was Auriel Bessemer; and the class philosopher, Ed Ingraham, dour, witty and unimpressed. He died in combat in World War II, probably questioning everything the army did. Once to illustrate in his column in *The Record* that people get what they deserve, this seventeen-year-old seer punctuated his essay with a quotation from Kipling: "They ate their fill of dead whale, and now blame the Gods for their bellyache."

On campus there were no drinking, smoking, or cars allowed, and only a few dances. For these they had their own orchestra (I played violin), which was good enough to be invited to give two radio concerts in 1926 and 1927 over WHK in Cleveland.

Mr. Boothby, as headmaster, had a weekly rap session

with the seniors, where they talked informally about religion, politics, and philosophy. Socratic-like, he led them along with questions. Once in a talk about religion, I said that we all had more religious feelings than we knew, because they were hidden under other feelings. Some of my peers laughed with derision at such an idea. Boothby paused a minute and then quietly rescued me, "Paul has said more than you realize." He then led us gently into insights about our own hidden selves.

Grant had a feeling of satisfaction at having found "the best in education", even though he and Lyla did without to accomplish it.

Chapter Thirty-Seven
The Final Years

The famous stock market crash of October, 1929, which started the great depression, did not disturb Grant at all. Because his speculations were about Heaven and not earth, he owned no stock at all. It was merely a spectacular event affecting somebody else. At first the depression was just called *Hard Times.* That had a cheerful ring. Just a little belt tightening that would do us good.

But something more ominous than hard times happened to America between 1929 and 1936. The old nostrums didn't work, and no one in authority could tell us why the essential vital metabolism of the nation pulsed slower and slower. As the nation's economic breath sank, a pallor spread over the land. As a college graduate desperately scratching out a living washing dishes, and trying not to go home defeated, I remember mostly the quiet of a dying nation in 1932. There were few customers in the stores, few cars on the road, and many silent industrial plants. The one consolation was that everything was dirt cheap, because in those days, when a depression came, prices actually went down, unlike today.

Between 1927 and 1932, Grant was in Cleveland in a succession of small churches in industrial neighborhoods — Union Ave., Collinwood, and Trinity on West Madison. As the depression deepened, his working class parishioners slipped deeper into poverty; and a note of desperation crept into his letters to me. I could see his spirit wither away as he tried to keep his churches and his family above water.

Yet he managed to save a little, and we borrowed, and worked so that Jack and I stayed in college. Such was his determination. In one letter he poured out his worries to me. His church had only paid him one-third of an already small salary. He had been sick and said that if anything happened to him, the small pension of a minister would hardly keep Lyla and my sisters, let alone educate them. That would be up to Jack and me. It was a sad letter.

Still I never heard a word of criticism of his people, for he knew their problems too. For a member faced with the foreclosure of his home, his pledge to the church was of minor importance. In 1932 there was no unemployment insurance or social security. Laissez faire frowned on such extravagance.

Even though I survived, I can never, even now, think of his letters in those days without pain and shame that I might have been the cause of his worries. Nor have I ever really forgiven America for the great depression and its frightful waste of human beings. For eight years before 1929, a mismanaged and venal economy simply beggered the working man and the farmer with low wages and low commodity prices, so that, when the depression came in earnest, the buying power of millions had no resilience. And a significant part of the profits from this squeeze had been poured into the speculative gambling den of the stock market.

At the peak of the so called "boom" in the summer of 1929, I earned thirty-five cents an hour in a ten-hour day at Thompson Products in Cleveland inspecting auto valves. Many of my fellow workers with families earned as low as fifty cents an hour.

But in 1935 things brightened a little for Grant. We had a happy time at my wedding to Blossom in the Shakespearean Garden at Mount Union College in June. And, in September, Grant was sent by the Methodist Conference to Willard, Ohio, to rescue a church and thirty-four worried members from foreclosure.

In the euphoria of the twenties, the Willard Methodists had proudly built a new church. But because the town banker had been skeptical of the security of a church (and rightly so, for, if the bank had to take it back, of what earthly rather than heavenly use was it?), thirty-four church members had personally obligated themselves to pay the debt. During the boom it seemed reasonable. Wasn't the stock market going to make us all rich? But in 1935 even their homes were being foreclosed.

So Grant's appointed task in his new charge was economic and not spiritual. He started vigorously with an organized campaign in the community and in the Conference. He interested the religion editor of the *Cleveland Plain Dealer* who did an article on his fight to save the homes of his members.

In his last letter to me in January, 1936, I felt his spirits revive and his confidence in himself flow again. He wrote happily; "We like Willard better than any place we have been. Mother (Lyla) is quite happy, and is a different woman. I don't blame her, for some of our churches had nothing at all."

I had told him about starting night law school, about our first happy Christmas, and about joining the First Methodist Church in Canton, Ohio. He especially liked the last news and felt a little better about my soul. A year before, when one defeat after another had been crowding in on me, he had written a poignant letter asking whether I had the faith to weather the storm.

He wrote then: "I can appreciate your feelings, for forty years ago unemployment forced me into the army. But that experience proved good for me. I had a deep religious background with a personal experience I came through with a clear vision. It was one of the griefs of my life that you have not experienced this. I am not blaming you, for you did not have a home. Since the beginning of high school, you have lived in a school, though I still think it was the best course."

But, in his last letter, he told me confidently that he was making real progress in lifting the debt from the backs of his people. Then, at home on Sunday morning, February 16, 1936, with a hopeful report in his hands to be announced at the church service that day, a coronary, his first and last, took his life.

I am glad there was some victory at the end. *The Cleveland Plain Dealer* reported: "The Rev. Mr. Perkins had attracted wide attention since going to the Willard church, through his efforts to raise $16,500 to clear a foreclosure on the church property and on the homes of thirty-four of its members who had signed the note. His report on Sunday was to account for $7,000 of that amount."

His death caused only a ripple or two. One came from an unexpected source. Fay Ashmun, a columnist and society editor for *The Alliance Review* in Alliance, Ohio, had reported the weddings of my brother Jack and me in June, 1935. After Grant's death she wrote in her column:

> *"Last summer when the trees were green, the air was warm, and the beauty of June lay on the land, I witnessed two wedding ceremonies within a few days of each other in which Rev. S. Grant Perkins assisted in the marriage of his two sons, Paul and Jack to two Alliance girls. Now, a little more than six months later, Rev. Perkins is dead, passing away in the saddle as every active man must wish to pass. I talked with him a little while last summer about the half sad joy of weddings and the problems of a minister and found, in that short time, a wholesome philosophy that must have been the foundation of his living."*

So it ended quietly as it had begun. His life melted into the universal human experience. I have only recaptured a breath or two of its fragrance, and have sensed only a tiny bit of its vitality and meaning.

Epilogue

Cotton and Meadow Creeks still meander peacefully between the hills of Whitley County, Kentucky. The rock spring where Grant carried water for his mother still trickles from the crevasses, but now serves no human need.

The crude log and frame churches that once housed a vibrant religion are gone.

Forts Sully and Niobrara are now only footnotes in American military history.

The courthouse and college at Barbourville, Kentucky, still grind out an important local brand of justice and education.

The Statendam, that sturdy Dutch ship that carried Grant to his first and last joyful adventure abroad, long ago was reduced to scrap. Ships of the air, as Grant foresaw in 1913, now make the Atlantic run.

Classical Leipzig survived the Prussian officer, World War I, Hitler, World War II and now, in East Germany, is garmented in an uncomfortable and unaccustomed proletariat straightjacket.

Rome seethes with political instability and energy, but the flexible and life-loving Italian survives and even prospers in a way. For all of the innocent zeal of its young minister in 1906, the church at 38 Via Firenza never did save Rome.

The Palestine that Grant saw through the words of his Bible is now the most dangerously radio-active spot in the world.

The towns we lived in and most of the churches he served still survive, Grant's life there now reduced to a line in a local church history.

I have dwelt on Grant's personal rather than his professional life because that is what I knew best. His sermons, I remember, were thoughtful rather than oratorical and evangelical, perhaps not very exciting to many congregations. He was a low key preacher, no Billy Sunday or Billy Graham, but I liked that best.

Between us there grew a subtle and mostly intellectual empathy. When, in 1932, I was in graduate school in English at The University of Pittsburgh, and my days blazed with intellectual excitement, he once said, almost wistfully, that one could realize ambitions in children. He had always wanted to be a writer and hoped that aspiration could be realized in me. It wasn't, of course, but I have been content with the law and the bench. They have been stimulating substitutes.

Grant's relationship to his children was old-fashioned and traditional, no hint of the grotesque family sitcom of television. But he was never purely authoritarian and gave us leeway to make our own mistakes. I remember no harsh or physical punishment, no applied razor straps to the posterior.

But I do remember biblical admonitions to walk the straight and narrow way. Once, when my brother Jack and I had quarreled and I had called him a nasty name, Grant solemnly and quietly told me of some Old Testament promise that whoever shall call his brother fool shall burn in hell. Boy, did that make an impression on my eleven year old conscience!

We had the normal father and son struggles for power and independence, but they were quiet rather than noisy affairs. Neither his authority nor my resistance were ever carried to extremes, perhaps because we both had a latent respect for the other.

In law there is a useful as well as a beautiful idea — the meeting of the minds. With a meeting of the minds, misunderstandings dissolve, hostility and anger subside, and our humanity returns.

I now know that he and I had a long meeting of the minds, even though never articulated or even openly acknowledged. Quite subtly, he taught me mind itself, which has to be of God, because it has no discernable physical anatomy.

So I return to the opening theme of this book — that the lives of ordinary Americans are a rich vein of story. Their names should not be forgotten.

And I find a biblical support in this.

> "There are some of them who have left a name
> So that men declare their praise.
> But there are some who have no memorial,
> Who have perished as though they had not lived.
> But these were men of mercy
> Whose righteous deeds have not been forgotten;

*Their prosperity will remain with their descendants
And their inheritance to their children's children.*"[87]

Footnotes and Sources

1. *Diary of a Geological Tour,* 1827-1828, Dr. Elisha Mitchell, University of North Carolina Press, 1905, page 24.
2. *Sources for the family history.* (1) *The Families of Ancient New Haven,* by Donald Jacobus, Clarence Smith And Co. New York 1927. (2) An unpublished manuscript by Dow Perkins, *The Genealogy of the Historic Tories of Old Wilkes County, North Carolina, Timothy and Joseph Perkins* in the Wilkesboro, N.C. library. (3)Other letters and sources cited in *The Genealogy And History of One Branch of the Perkins Family in America* by the author Paul M. Perkins on file in the Library of Congress and other state libraries. (Call number CS71.P45/1980). Source for the Benjamin Cleveland story, page 11, *King's Mountain And Its Heroes,* by Draper 1915 Pg. 437 Source for the affair at Draper's Meadows, page 14. *The Wilderness Road* by Robert Kincaid 1947 Bobbs-Merrill Page 57
3. *Election Statistics for Whitley Co. Kentucky,* a typed manuscript in The Cleveland Public Library 4
4. The Frank Faulkner story is from a manuscript dated about 1929 by a son, Judge Henry Cook Faulkner, deceased, in the possession of a granddaughter Maureen Faulkner of Berea, Kentucky.
5. *Yosemite National Park,* David McKay 1967
6. "Incident On the Isthmus" by John C. Kennedy *American Heritage Magazine* June 1968
7. *History of American Methodism,* Abington Press, Vol 2, Page 94
8. This and a following quotation are from *The Discipline of The Methodist Episcopal Church* 1884 Courtesy Rev. Howard Wiant, Lakeside, Ohio.
9. *50 Reasons For Becoming A Methodist* by N. B. Cooksey, Western Methodist Book Concern, 1881 Page 26. courtesy Howard Wiant
10. See note 4, Judge Henry Cook Faulkner manuscript
11. For the history of the Methodist Church see note 7. For background on the coal and timber industries, *Night Comes to the Cumberlands* Harry Caudill, *Atlantic Monthly Press,* 1962.
12. *The Prairie Years,* by Carl Sandburg, Harcourt Brace, 1926, Page 30.
13. I can understand Grant's pleasure with his muzzle loader. My son, Paul Grant, has since high school days owned a real muzzle-loaded rifle. Its long, octagonal barrel was heavy and steady in your hand. The stock was polished walnut and shining brass. It fired with a crisp, clean sound and was quite accurate on target. Under my son's stern directions, I was sometimes allowed to fire it.
14. *The Southern Highlander* by John C. Campbell, University of Kentucky Press 1969 Page 6 (original: Russell Sage Foundation, 1921) used with permission
15. For general background on life in the Kentucky mountains (1)" Night Comes to the Cumberlands,"*Atlantic Monthly Press,* Harry Caudill 1962

(2)*The Wilderness Road* by Robert Kincaid Bobbs Merill 1947 (3) *The Southern Highlander And His Home* John C. Campbell, University of Kentucky Press 1969 (4) *The Spirit Of The Mountains* Emma Bell Miles, facsimile edition, University of Tennessee Press, 1975 (5) *Our Southern Highlander* by Horace Kephart, McMillen, 1913; University of Tennessee Press, 1969.

16. All quotations an this chapter are from the *Youth's Companion* 1886-1888 in the Stark County, Ohio, District Library at Canton, Ohio

17. All quotations in this chapter are from an article by James Lane Allen in the June 1886 issue of the *Harpers New Monthly Magazine.*

18. From a letter written by James B. Faulkner to the author in 1940.

19. For information about Chicago at that time. *Clarence Darrow For The Defense,* Irving Stone, 1943. There is perhaps an apocryphal story about Darrow. He had gone to Chicago in the first place because he had told a nosy matron in Kinsman, Ohio, where he had started practice, that he had a big case in Chicago. He had to go to make the story look true. He liked Chicago so well, he stayed.

20. Information as to the enlistment record and the monthly reports about Company A came from James B. Rhoads, archivist of the United States in 1973 and 1974.

21. Many details of life at Fort Sully are from the monthly reports of the Fort Commander on deposit at the South Dakota Historical Society, Pierre. Also the manuscript of the Master's thesis of Steven Hockman on the history of Fort Sully. The story of the bandmaster Achille LaGuardia is from the latter source.

22. Ironically, the Ghost Dance of the western Indians had its origins in a primitive Christianity. Originating with the Paiutes of Nevada in 1888, the basis was a belief in an Indian Messiah, Wovoka. It was believed that this Messiah would cover the earth with new grass, buffalo, and horses. Those who danced the Ghost Dance wore ghostshirts and would be saved for the new day. The shirts would protect them from bluecoat's bullets. The movement spread rapidly but was never warlike. It was semi-religious and ceremonial only. The Americans completely misunderstood the movement as promising new wars. It was in this atmosphere of hysteria that the massacre at Wounded Knee took place. The Ghost Dances were the last spasmodic convulsion of the Plains Indians (Concise Dictionary of American History, Scribners 1962 Page 400)

A typical report of Wounded Knee in the American press was the Canton, Ohio, *Repository's* headline: "Now There Are 300 'Good Indians'."

23. *The Sioux Of The Rosebud: A History In Pictures* by Henry and Jean Tyree Hamilton, University of Oklahoma Press, 1971, Page 6. This book features the work of photographer John Anderson of Valentine, Nebraska, who worked and photographed the Indians near Fort Niobrara. Some of his pictures are included in this book. This permission does not include any part of the selection independently copyrighted or bearing a separate source notation. The responsibility for determining the source of the material is with the prospective publisher.

24. Micro film records of the *Valentine Republican* in the Nebraska State

Historical Society, Lincoln, Nebraska. 25

25. Footnote 21

26. *Vanished Arizona: Recollections Of My Army Life* by Martha Summerhayes, Philadelphia, 1908 copy in the Nebraska State Historical Society, Lincoln, Nebraska, Page 290

27. All the quotations on pages 56 are from the Summerhayes book. (See note 26) Pages 280, 285,and 288

28. The detailed story of Union College is found in *Union College* by Erwin Bradley, Barbourville, Ky. 1954

29. *Abraham Lincoln, The Prairie Years Vol.I* by Carl Sandburg, Harcourt Brace 1926 Page 264 copyright renewed by Carl Sandburg 1954, used with permission of Harcourt Brace Jovanovich, Inc.

30. Ibid Page 264

31. Ibid Page 261

32. Ibid Page 216

33. Ibid Page 266

34. Ibid Page 269

35. *Platforms of the Great Political Parties, 1856-1912* by South Trimble, Clerk of the House of Representatives, July 1912. (In my personal library) Pages 96 and 102

36. *The Spanish War, A Compact History,* Keller. Hawthorne Press, 1960, Page 18, E. P. Dutton.

37. *In The Days of McKinley,* Margaret Leech. Harper & Row. 1959. Page 181

38. See footnote 20

39. See footnote 20

40. *The Spanish War* by Russell Alger (then Secretary of War), Harpers, 1911, Page 18, and for other details of that war.

41. See footnote 20

42. *The Rough Riders* by Theodore Roosevelt, Charles Scribner and Sons, complete edition 1926. Vol XI Pg 7

43. From a drover and tavern keeper. Daniel Drew first became a money lender, then a Wall Street figure who took over the Erie Railroad, when it defaulted on his loans. He used it as a milk cow to finance many questionable projects. But he became a cropper when he joined with the infamous Jay Gould in a fight with the Vanderbilts. But before he was ruined, he did found Drew Seminary. *(History of Great American Fortunes,* Gustavus Myers, 1907)

44. *Year Book, Drew Theological Seminary,* 1903-10

45. Roosevelt coined this famous phrase in 1906 according to most dictionaries. For background about New York in 1905, I used *Our Times, The Turn of the Century,* Mark Sullivan, Scribners, 1926, and *This Fabulous Century,* 1900-1910, Time-Life

46. *This Fabulous Century* Page 244

47. Information about the Statendam and a photograph of it came from John Lochead of The Mariner's Museum, Newport News, Va., in 1975 after many years of false leads trying to find out what ship my father sailed on May 5, 1905. He also sent me the rate schedule.

48. From an article "Saxon Methodism" in the *Methodist Review,* January, 1906, by U.S. Grant Perkins (In The Library of Congress)

49. *This Hallowed Ground* by Bruce Catton, Doubleday and Company, New York, 1955, Page 3 used with permission

50. All information and quotations in this chapter about Bishop William Burt are from his unpublished journals in the United Methodist Archives, Box 488, Lake Junaluska, North Carolina, and are used with permission. (Letter June 1, 1976)

51. See Note 48. Subsequent quotations in this chapter are from tha same article.

52. An article "The Passing of The Alps" by U.S. Grant Perkins in *The Methodist Review,* New York, March, 1909. All the subsequent quotations in this chapter are from the same article. I also found five other articles by Grant in the same magazine, previously unknown to me.

53. *Encyclopedia of American History,* editor Richard Morris, Harper Bros., 1953, Vol. 1, Page 269

54. Information on the Methodist Center in Rome is from the *Encyclopedia of World Methodism,* Abingdon Press, Pages 1239-1242 and from material in the papers of Bishop William Burt. (See footnote 50)

55. See page 138, Chapter Twenty-seven

56. An economic footnote. When I was in Rome in 1969, the taxi fare from the station to the hotel, for a new tourist, was 1400 lira. But the fare from the hotel to the station, for the experienced tourist, was only 700 lira. All the quotations in this chapter are from my father's diary.

57. *Today In Palestine* by Dunning Page 96 (Stark County, Ohio, District Library)

58. See Note 57

59. *Today In Palestine* by Dunning Page 72

60. *The Bible As History* by Werner Keller

61. *Today In Palestine* Note 57 Page 46

62. *The Land That Was Lost* by Treves, Dutton 1912 Page 36

63. Adler's *Directory of Steamship Landings* has the *Romanic* arriving in Boston from Italian ports on July 4, 1906. (My letter from Edwin Sanford, Boston Public Library August 28, 1975)

64. Now Trinity Temple a combination church and apartment complex for the elderly. It had been Fanny Henning Speed's church when she helped finance the start of Union College. (See Chapter 11)

65. The cornerstone of his new church was laid after he had left for Michigan. A sturdy brick church, it is still filled on Sunday, despite its location in central city Covington. The plain where the Latonia Race track once reverberated to the roars of horse racing fans is now empty, two blocks from the church. The track has been moved to suburbia. In September, 1982, I was permitted to read this chapter to the congregation. It was quite a thrill to stand in the pulpit where my father had stood 76 years before.

66. History of Onaway, Michigan, is from its Jubilee program of 1974

67. Interview with Maybelle Roberts in October, 1977.

68. Interview with Grace Prestiger, October, 1977. I also thank Mrs. Elma Gay, librarian at Onaway, Michigan, for local history and for steering me to

interviews with two 90-year-old residents.

69. *The Catholic Citizen* of Milwaukee as reported in *The Literary Digest.* Bishop Burt's papers, note 50

70. See note 50. In the collection of Bishop Burt's papers is an extensive collection of newspaper clippings about the Roosevelt-Vatican incident. All quotations on this subject in this chapter are from this collection.

71. From *The Methodist Review* July, 1910, Page 590 in The Library of Congress.

72. How do I know that Grant got a Ford before 1916? His "Flivver" had a brass radiator. Ford eliminated the brass for a plain black after 1916.

73. In 1900 there were 10 miles of concrete road in the country, but by 1925, 20,000. *Our Times, The Turn of the Century,* by Mark Sullivan, Charles Scribner's and Sons, 1926, P. 63.

74. "The New Industrial Era" in the September, 1914, issue of *The Methodist Review,* by Grant Perkins. All subsequent quotations in this chapter are from the same article.

75. *Our Times,* by Mark Sullivan, Scribner's, Page 147

76. *The Common Law* O. W. Holmes Jr, Little, Brown and Co., 1881, page 41. From a first edition in my library.

77. *Vanished Arizona,* page 282. See footnote 26.

78. "Prohibition And The Future" by Grant Perkins. *The Methodist Review,* January 1917 Page 115

79. I have a unique way of verifying the German superiority in small arms then. My son Paul Grant, as a gun collector, once owned a German Mausser and an American Krag of about the year 1870. The Mausser was an eight shot repeater, but the Krag still shot one bullet at a time.

80. *Concise Dictionary of American History,* Scribner, 1961, page 1045.

81. Minutes of the Board of Trustees of Antioch College, February 7, 1919. Courtesy Nina Myatt, Historian of Antioch College.

82. *Woodrow Wilson* by Gerald Johnson, Harper Bros., 1944, page 178.

83. Ibid. page 267.

84. Ibid. page 256.

85. *Hardscrabble Hellas* by Lucien Price, Atlantic Monthly, February 1927: © 1927 by Lucien Price reprinted with permission.

86. Ibid.

87. *Ecclesiasticus* 44: 1-4ac, 5-9ab, 10-11, 1315 One of the intertestamentary books of the Bible, no longer in most Bibles.

88. "Western Star" by Stephen Vincent Benet, Holt, Rhinart, and Winston Inc. copyright 1943 by Rosemary Carr Benet copyright renewed (c) 1971 by Rachel Benet Lewis, Thomas C. Benet, and Stephanie Benet Mahin. Reprinted permission of Brandt and Brandt, Literary Agents, Inc. From the invocation.

I acknowledge the services of Susan Swain, Mary Holland, Karen Bishop, and Mildred Huntley in typing this manuscript at its various stages.